Just The

facts101
Textbook Key Facts

Textbook Outlines, Highlights, and Practice Quizzes

Intro Stats

by Richard D. De Veaux, 4th Edition

All "Just the Facts101" Material Written or Prepared by Cram101 Textbook Reviews

Title Page

STUDYING MADE EASY

This Facts101 notebook is designed to make studying easier and increase your comprehension of the textbook material. Instead of starting with a blank notebook and trying to write down everything discussed in class lectures, you can use this Facts101 textbook notebook and annotate your notes along with the lecture.

Our goal is to give you the best tools for success.

For a supreme understanding of the course, pair your notebook with our online tools. Should you decide you prefer jtfl01.com as your study tool,

we'd like to offer you a trade...

Our Trade In program is a simple way for us to keep our promise and provide you the best studying tools, regardless of where you purchased your Facts101 textbook notebook. As long as your notebook is in *Like New Condition**, you can send it back to us and we will immediately give you a JustTheFacts101.com account free for 120 days!

Let The *Trade In* Begin!

THREE SIMPLE STEPS TO TRADE:

1. Go to www.jtf101.com/tradein and fill out the packing slip information.

2. Submit and print the packing slip and mail it in with your Facts101 textbook notebook.

3. Activate your account after you receive your email confirmation.

* Books must be returned in *Like New Condition*, meaning there is no damage to the book including, but not limited to; ripped or torn pages, markings or writing on pages, or folded / creased pages. Upon receiving the book, Facts101 will inspect it and reserves the right to terminate your free Facts101.com account and return your textbook notebook at the owners expense.

LEARNING SYSTEM

"Just the Facts101" is a Content Technologies publication and tool designed to give you all the facts from your textbooks. Visit JustTheFacts101.com for the full practice test for each of your chapters for virtually any of your textbooks.

Facts101 has built custom study tools specific to your textbook. We provide all of the factual testable information and unlike traditional study guides, we will never send you back to your textbook for more information.

YOU WILL NEVER HAVE TO HIGHLIGHT A BOOK AGAIN!

Facts101 StudyGuides
All of the information in this StudyGuide is written specifically for your textbook. We include the key terms, places, people, and concepts... the information you can expect on your next exam!

Want to take a practice test?
Throughout each chapter of this StudyGuide you will find links to JustTheFacts101.com where you can select specific chapters to take a complete test on, or you can subscribe and get practice tests for up to 12 of your textbooks, along with other exclusive Jtf101.com tools like problem solving labs and reference libraries.

JustTheFacts101.com
Only Jtf101.com gives you the outlines, highlights, and PRACTICE TESTS specific to your textbook. JustTheFacts101.com is an online application where you'll discover study tools designed to make the most of your limited study time.

By purchasing this book, you get 50% off the normal monthly subscription fee!. Just enter the promotional code **'DK73DW25201'** on the Jtf101.com registration screen.

www.JustTheFacts101.com

ISBN(s): 9781497014428. PUBE-7.2014618

Intro Stats
Richard D. De Veaux, 4th

CONTENTS

1. Stats Starts Here 5
2. Displaying and Describing Categorical Data 11
3. Displaying and Summarizing Quantitative Data 17
4. Understanding and Comparing Distributions 25
5. The Standard Deviation as a Ruler and the Normal Model 30
6. Scatterplots, Association, and Correlation 36
7. Linear Regression 43
8. Regression Wisdom 51
9. Understanding Randomness 57
10. Sample Surveys 62
11. From Randomness to Probability 73
12. Probability Rules! 79
13. Random Variables and Probability Models 85
14. Sampling Distribution Models 93
15. Confidence Intervals for Proportions 101
16. Testing Hypotheses About Proportions 108
17. Inferences About Means 115
18. More About Tests and Intervals 125
19. Comparing Groups 133
20. Paired Samples and Blocks 142
21. Comparing Counts 149
22. Inferences for Regression 157

1. Stats Starts Here

CHAPTER OUTLINE: KEY TERMS, PEOPLE, PLACES, CONCEPTS

_____	Bias
_____	Population
_____	Sample
_____	Independence
_____	Identifier
_____	Measurement
_____	Distribution

CHAPTER HIGHLIGHTS & NOTES: KEY TERMS, PEOPLE, PLACES, CONCEPTS

Bias	Bias is an inclination of temperament or outlook to present or hold a partial perspective and a refusal to even consider the possible merits of alternative points of view. People may be biased toward or against an individual, a race, a religion, a social class, or a political party. Biased means one-sided, lacking a neutral viewpoint, not having an open mind.
Population	A statistical population is a set of individuals or objects of interest.

A subset of a population is called a subpopulation. If different subpopulations have different properties, so the overall population is heterogeneous, the properties and response of the overall population can often be better understood if it is first separated into distinct subpopulations. For instance, a particular medicine may have different effects on different subpopulations, and these effects may be obscured or dismissed if such special subpopulations are not identified and examined in isolation.

Similarly, one can often estimate parameters more accurately if one separates out subpopulations: the distribution of heights among people is better modeled by considering men and women as separate subpopulations, for instance. |
| Sample | In statistics and quantitative research methodology, a data sample is a set of data collected and/or selected from a statistical population by a defined procedure. |

1. Stats Starts Here

Independence	In probability theory, to say that two events are independent means that the occurrence of one does not affect the probability of the other. Similarly, two random variables are independent if the realization of one does not affect the probability distribution of the other. The concept of independence extends to dealing with collections of more than two events or random variables.
Identifier	An identifier is a name that identifies either a unique object or a unique class of objects, where the 'object' or class may be an idea, physical [countable] object (or class thereof), or physical [noncountable] substance (or class thereof). The abbreviation ID often refers to identity, identification (the process of identifying), or an identifier. An identifier may be a word, number, letter, symbol, or any combination of those.
Measurement	Measurement is the assignment of numbers to objects or events. It is a cornerstone of most natural sciences, technology, economics, and quantitative research in other social sciences. Any measurement can be judged by the following meta-measurement criteria values: level of measurement dimensions (units), and uncertainty.
Distribution	In algebra and number theory, a distribution is a function on a system of finite sets into an abelian group which is analogous to an integral: it is thus the algebraic analogue of a distribution in the sense of generalised function. The original examples of distributions occur, unnamed, as functions f on Q/Z satisfying $$\sum_{r=0}^{N-1} \phi\left(x + \frac{r}{N}\right) = \phi(Nx).$$ We shall call these ordinary distributions. They also occur in p-adic integration theory in Iwasawa theory.

1. Stats Starts Here

1. _____ is an inclination of temperament or outlook to present or hold a partial perspective and a refusal to even consider the possible merits of alternative points of view. People may be biased toward or against an individual, a race, a religion, a social class, or a political party. Biased means one-sided, lacking a neutral viewpoint, not having an open mind.

   a. Covariance
   b. Bias
   c. Law of total cumulance
   d. Law of total expectation

2. In probability theory, to say that two events are independent means that the occurrence of one does not affect the probability of the other. Similarly, two random variables are independent if the realization of one does not affect the probability distribution of the other.

   The concept of _____ extends to dealing with collections of more than two events or random variables.

   a. Independence
   b. B-convex space
   c. Bean machine
   d. Chain rule

3. A statistical _____ is a set of individuals or objects of interest.

   A subset of a _____ is called a sub_____. If different sub_____s have different properties, so the overall _____ is heterogeneous, the properties and response of the overall _____ can often be better understood if it is first separated into distinct sub_____s. For instance, a particular medicine may have different effects on different sub_____s, and these effects may be obscured or dismissed if such special sub_____s are not identified and examined in isolation.

   Similarly, one can often estimate parameters more accurately if one separates out sub_____s: the distribution of heights among people is better modeled by considering men and women as separate sub_____s, for instance.

   a. Ceiling effect
   b. Population
   c. Consistency
   d. Cost-of-living index

4. . An _____ is a name that identifies either a unique object or a unique class of objects, where the 'object' or class may be an idea, physical [countable] object (or class thereof), or physical [noncountable] substance (or class thereof). The abbreviation ID often refers to identity, identification (the process of identifying), or an _____. An _____ may be a word, number, letter, symbol, or any combination of those.

   a. Binary object
   b. CcREL

c. CD-Text

d. Identifier

5. In statistics and quantitative research methodology, a data _____ is a set of data collected and/or selected from a statistical population by a defined procedure.

a. Sample

b. Deep sampling

c. Judgment sample

d. Lot quality assurance sampling

1. b
2. a
3. b
4. d
5. a

You can take the complete Chapter Practice Test

for 1. Stats Starts Here
on all key terms, persons, places, and concepts.

Online 99 Cents

http://www.JustTheFacts101.com

Use www.JustTheFacts101.com for all your study needs

including Facts101's online interactive problem solving labs in

chemistry, statistics, mathematics, and more.

2. Displaying and Describing Categorical Data

CHAPTER OUTLINE: KEY TERMS, PEOPLE, PLACES, CONCEPTS

	Data analysis
	Distribution
	Regression
	Condition
	Independence
	Bias
	Sample
	SIMPLE

CHAPTER HIGHLIGHTS & NOTES: KEY TERMS, PEOPLE, PLACES, CONCEPTS

Data analysis

Analysis of data is a process of inspecting, cleaning, transforming, and modeling data with the goal of discovering useful information, suggesting conclusions, and supporting decision making. Data analysis has multiple facets and approaches, encompassing diverse techniques under a variety of names, in different business, science, and social science domains.

Data mining is a particular data analysis technique that focuses on modeling and knowledge discovery for predictive rather than purely descriptive purposes.

Distribution

In algebra and number theory, a distribution is a function on a system of finite sets into an abelian group which is analogous to an integral: it is thus the algebraic analogue of a distribution in the sense of generalised function.

The original examples of distributions occur, unnamed, as functions f on Q/Z

satisfying $\sum_{r=0}^{N-1} \phi\left(x + \frac{r}{N}\right) = \phi(Nx)$.

We shall call these ordinary distributions.

2. Displaying and Describing Categorical Data

Regression	Regression in medicine is a characteristic of diseases to show lighter symptoms without completely disappearing. At a later point, symptoms may return. These symptoms are then called recidive.
Condition	Comprehensive treatment of the word 'condition' requires emphasizing that it is ambiguous in the sense of having multiple normal meanings and that its meanings are often vague in the sense of admitting borderline cases. According to the 2007 American Philosophy: an Encyclopedia, in one widely used sense, conditions are or resemble qualities, properties, features, characteristics, or attributes. In these senses, a condition is often denoted by a nominalization of a grammatical predicate: 'being equilateral' is a nominalization of the predicate 'is equilateral'.
Independence	In probability theory, to say that two events are independent means that the occurrence of one does not affect the probability of the other. Similarly, two random variables are independent if the realization of one does not affect the probability distribution of the other. The concept of independence extends to dealing with collections of more than two events or random variables.
Bias	Bias is an inclination of temperament or outlook to present or hold a partial perspective and a refusal to even consider the possible merits of alternative points of view. People may be biased toward or against an individual, a race, a religion, a social class, or a political party. Biased means one-sided, lacking a neutral viewpoint, not having an open mind.
Sample	In statistics and quantitative research methodology, a data sample is a set of data collected and/or selected from a statistical population by a defined procedure.
SIMPLE	The Standard Interface for Multiple Platform Link Evaluation (SIMPLE) is a military communications protocol defined in NATO's Standardization Agreement 5602.

2. Displaying and Describing Categorical Data

1. The Standard Interface for Multiple Platform Link Evaluation (_____) is a military communications protocol defined in NATO's Standardization Agreement 5602.

   a. Battle lab
   b. SIMPLE
   c. Benefit financing model
   d. Capability

2. In algebra and number theory, a _____ is a function on a system of finite sets into an abelian group which is analogous to an integral: it is thus the algebraic analogue of a _____ in the sense of generalised function.

   The original examples of _____s occur, unnamed, as functions f on Q/Z

   $$\sum_{r=0}^{N-1} \phi\left(x + \frac{r}{N}\right) = \phi(Nx) \ .$$
   satisfying

   We shall call these ordinary _____s. They also occur in p-adic integration theory in Iwasawa theory.

   a. Binomial
   b. Canonical form
   c. Closed-form expression
   d. Distribution

3. Analysis of data is a process of inspecting, cleaning, transforming, and modeling data with the goal of discovering useful information, suggesting conclusions, and supporting decision making. _____ has multiple facets and approaches, encompassing diverse techniques under a variety of names, in different business, science, and social science domains.

   Data mining is a particular _____ technique that focuses on modeling and knowledge discovery for predictive rather than purely descriptive purposes.

   a. Covariance
   b. Law of total covariance
   c. Law of total cumulance
   d. Data analysis

4. _____ in medicine is a characteristic of diseases to show lighter symptoms without completely disappearing. At a later point, symptoms may return. These symptoms are then called recidive.

   a. 1947 New York City smallpox outbreak
   b. 1993 Four Corners hantavirus outbreak
   c. Regression
   d. 2012 Middle East respiratory syndrome coronavirus outbreak

5. Comprehensive treatment of the word '_____' requires emphasizing that it is ambiguous in the sense of having multiple normal meanings and that its meanings are often vague in the sense of admitting borderline cases.

    According to the 2007 American Philosophy: an Encyclopedia, in one widely used sense, _____s are or resemble qualities, properties, features, characteristics, or attributes. In these senses, a _____ is often denoted by a nominalization of a grammatical predicate: 'being equilateral' is a nominalization of the predicate 'is equilateral'.

    a. Condition
    b. Boolean network
    c. Canon
    d. Ceqli

1. b
2. d
3. d
4. c
5. a

You can take the complete Chapter Practice Test

for 2. Displaying and Describing Categorical Data
on all key terms, persons, places, and concepts.

Online 99 Cents

http://www.JustTheFacts101.com

Use www.JustTheFacts101.com for all your study needs

including Facts101's online interactive problem solving labs in

chemistry, statistics, mathematics, and more.

3. Displaying and Summarizing Quantitative Data

CHAPTER OUTLINE: KEY TERMS, PEOPLE, PLACES, CONCEPTS

_____ Condition

_____ Data analysis

_____ Bimodal distribution

_____ Mode

_____ Multimodal distribution

_____ Uniform distribution

_____ Bimodal

_____ Theorem

_____ Distribution

_____ Interquartile range

_____ Median

_____ Range

_____ Mean

_____ T-test

_____ Standard deviation

_____ Variance

_____ Correlation

_____ Independence

_____ Rounding

3. Displaying and Summarizing Quantitative Data

Condition	Comprehensive treatment of the word 'condition' requires emphasizing that it is ambiguous in the sense of having multiple normal meanings and that its meanings are often vague in the sense of admitting borderline cases. According to the 2007 American Philosophy: an Encyclopedia, in one widely used sense, conditions are or resemble qualities, properties, features, characteristics, or attributes. In these senses, a condition is often denoted by a nominalization of a grammatical predicate: 'being equilateral' is a nominalization of the predicate 'is equilateral'.
Data analysis	Analysis of data is a process of inspecting, cleaning, transforming, and modeling data with the goal of discovering useful information, suggesting conclusions, and supporting decision making. Data analysis has multiple facets and approaches, encompassing diverse techniques under a variety of names, in different business, science, and social science domains. Data mining is a particular data analysis technique that focuses on modeling and knowledge discovery for predictive rather than purely descriptive purposes.
Bimodal distribution	In statistics, a bimodal distribution is a continuous probability distribution with two different modes. These appear as distinct peaks (local maxima) in the probability density function. More generally, a multimodal distribution is a continuous probability distribution with two or more modes..
Mode	The mode is the value that appears most often in a set of data. The mode of a discrete probability distribution is the value x at which its probability mass function takes its maximum value. In other words, it is the value that is most likely to be sampled.
Multimodal distribution	In statistics, a multimodal distribution is a continuous probability distribution with two or more modes.
Uniform distribution	In probability theory and statistics, the continuous uniform distribution or rectangular distribution is a family of symmetric probability distributions such that for each member of the family, all intervals of the same length on the distribution's support are equally probable. The support is defined by the two parameters, a and b, which are its minimum and maximum values. The distribution is often abbreviated U(a,b).
Bimodal	In statistics, a bimodal distribution is a continuous probability distribution with two different modes. These appear as distinct peaks (local maxima) in the probability density function. More generally, a multimodal distribution is a continuous probability distribution with two or more modes.

3. Displaying and Summarizing Quantitative Data

CHAPTER HIGHLIGHTS & NOTES: KEY TERMS, PEOPLE, PLACES, CONCEPTS

Theorem	In mathematics, a theorem is a statement that has been proven on the basis of previously established statements, such as other theorems--and generally accepted statements, such as axioms. The proof of a mathematical theorem is a logical argument for the theorem statement given in accord with the rules of a deductive system. The proof of a theorem is often interpreted as justification of the truth of the theorem statement.
Distribution	In algebra and number theory, a distribution is a function on a system of finite sets into an abelian group which is analogous to an integral: it is thus the algebraic analogue of a distribution in the sense of generalised function.

The original examples of distributions occur, unnamed, as functions f on Q/Z

$$\text{satisfying } \sum_{r=0}^{N-1} \phi\left(x + \frac{r}{N}\right) = \phi(Nx) \ .$$

We shall call these ordinary distributions. They also occur in p-adic integration theory in Iwasawa theory.

Interquartile range	In statistics, the interdecile range is the difference between the first and the ninth deciles . The interdecile range is a measure of statistical dispersion of the values in a set of data, similar to the range and the interquartile range, and can be computed from the (non-parametric) seven-number summary.

Despite its simplicity, for estimating the standard deviation of a normal distribution, the scaled interdecile range gives a reasonably efficient estimator.

Median	In statistics and probability theory, the median is the numerical value separating the higher half of a data sample, a population, or a probability distribution, from the lower half. The median of a finite list of numbers can be found by arranging all the observations from lowest value to highest value and picking the middle one (e.g., the median of {3, 3, 5, 9, 11} is 5). If there is an even number of observations, then there is no single middle value; the median is then usually defined to be the mean of the two middle values (the median of {3, 5, 7, 9} is (5 + 7) / 2 = 6), which corresponds to interpreting the median as the fully trimmed mid-range.
Range	In arithmetic, the range of a set of data is the difference between the largest and smallest values.

However, in descriptive statistics, this concept of range has a more complex meaning. The range is the size of the smallest interval which contains all the data and provides an indication of statistical dispersion.

3. Displaying and Summarizing Quantitative Data

Mean	In probability and statistics, mean and expected value are used synonymously to refer to one measure of the central tendency either of a probability distribution or of the random variable characterized by that distribution. In the case of a discrete probability distribution of a random variable X, the mean is equal to the sum over every possible value weighted by the probability of that value; that is, it is computed by taking the product of each possible value x of X and its probability P(x), and then adding all these products together, giving $$\mu = \sum x P(x)$$.
T-test	A t-test is any statistical hypothesis test in which the test statistic follows a Student's t distribution if the null hypothesis is supported. It can be used to determine if two sets of data are significantly different from each other, and is most commonly applied when the test statistic would follow a normal distribution if the value of a scaling term in the test statistic were known. When the scaling term is unknown and is replaced by an estimate based on the data, the test statistic (under certain conditions) follows a Student's t distribution.
Standard deviation	In statistics and probability theory, the standard deviation shows how much variation or dispersion from the average exists. A low standard deviation indicates that the data points tend to be very close to the mean (also called expected value); a high standard deviation indicates that the data points are spread out over a large range of values. The standard deviation of a random variable, statistical population, data set, or probability distribution is the square root of its variance.
Variance	In probability theory and statistics, variance measures how far a set of numbers is spread out. (A variance of zero indicates that all the values are identical). Variance is always non-negative: A small variance indicates that the data points tend to be very close to the mean (expected value) and hence to each other, while a high variance indicates that the data points are very spread out from the mean and from each other.
Correlation	In statistics, dependence is any statistical relationship between two random variables or two sets of data. Correlation refers to any of a broad class of statistical relationships involving dependence. Familiar examples of dependent phenomena include the correlation between the physical statures of parents and their offspring, and the correlation between the demand for a product and its price.
Independence	In probability theory, to say that two events are independent means that the occurrence of one does not affect the probability of the other. Similarly, two random variables are independent if the realization of one does not affect the probability distribution of the other.

3. Displaying and Summarizing Quantitative Data

Rounding	Rounding a numerical value means replacing it by another value that is approximately equal but has a shorter, simpler, or more explicit representation; for example, replacing £23.4476 with £23.45, or the fraction 312/937 with 1/3, or the expression v2 with 1.414.
	Rounding is often done on purpose to obtain a value that is easier to write and handle than the original. It may be done also to indicate the accuracy of a computed number; for example, a quantity that was computed as 123,456 but is known to be accurate only to within a few hundred units is better stated as 'about 123,500.'
	On the other hand, rounding introduces some round-off error in the result.

1. In statistics, the interdecile range is the difference between the first and the ninth deciles . The interdecile range is a measure of statistical dispersion of the values in a set of data, similar to the range and the _____, and can be computed from the (non-parametric) seven-number summary.

   Despite its simplicity, for estimating the standard deviation of a normal distribution, the scaled interdecile range gives a reasonably efficient estimator.

   a. Geometric standard deviation
   b. Interquartile range
   c. Harmonic mean
   d. Weighted arithmetic mean

2. In mathematics, a _____ is a statement that has been proven on the basis of previously established statements, such as other _____s--and generally accepted statements, such as axioms. The proof of a mathematical _____ is a logical argument for the _____ statement given in accord with the rules of a deductive system. The proof of a _____ is often interpreted as justification of the truth of the _____ statement.

   a. Theorem
   b. Propositional formula
   c. Propositional function
   d. Rule of inference

3. . Analysis of data is a process of inspecting, cleaning, transforming, and modeling data with the goal of discovering useful information, suggesting conclusions, and supporting decision making. _____ has multiple facets and approaches, encompassing diverse techniques under a variety of names, in different business, science, and social science domains.

Data mining is a particular _____ technique that focuses on modeling and knowledge discovery for predictive rather than purely descriptive purposes.

a. Covariance
b. Data analysis
c. Law of total cumulance
d. Law of total expectation

4. Comprehensive treatment of the word '_____' requires emphasizing that it is ambiguous in the sense of having multiple normal meanings and that its meanings are often vague in the sense of admitting borderline cases.

    According to the 2007 American Philosophy: an Encyclopedia, in one widely used sense, _____s are or resemble qualities, properties, features, characteristics, or attributes. In these senses, a _____ is often denoted by a nominalization of a grammatical predicate: 'being equilateral' is a nominalization of the predicate 'is equilateral'.

    a. Belief revision
    b. Condition
    c. Canon
    d. Ceqli

5. In probability theory and statistics, the continuous _____ or rectangular distribution is a family of symmetric probability distributions such that for each member of the family, all intervals of the same length on the distribution's support are equally probable. The support is defined by the two parameters, a and b, which are its minimum and maximum values. The distribution is often abbreviated U(a,b).

    a. Bates distribution
    b. Benini distribution
    c. Uniform distribution
    d. Beta distribution

1. b
2. a
3. b
4. b
5. c

You can take the complete Chapter Practice Test

for 3. Displaying and Summarizing Quantitative Data
on all key terms, persons, places, and concepts.

Online 99 Cents

http://www.JustTheFacts101.com

Use www.JustTheFacts101.com for all your study needs

including Facts101's online interactive problem solving labs in

chemistry, statistics, mathematics, and more.

4. Understanding and Comparing Distributions

CHAPTER OUTLINE: KEY TERMS, PEOPLE, PLACES, CONCEPTS

	Analysis
	Data analysis
	Standard deviation
	Exponential smoothing
	Moving average

CHAPTER HIGHLIGHTS & NOTES: KEY TERMS, PEOPLE, PLACES, CONCEPTS

Analysis	Analysis is the process of breaking a complex topic or substance into smaller parts to gain a better understanding of it. The technique has been applied in the study of mathematics and logic since before Aristotle (384-322 B.C)., though analysis as a formal concept is a relatively recent development.
	The word comes from the Ancient Greek ?????s?? (analusis, 'a breaking up', from ana- 'up, throughout' and lysis 'a loosening').
Data analysis	Analysis of data is a process of inspecting, cleaning, transforming, and modeling data with the goal of discovering useful information, suggesting conclusions, and supporting decision making. Data analysis has multiple facets and approaches, encompassing diverse techniques under a variety of names, in different business, science, and social science domains.
	Data mining is a particular data analysis technique that focuses on modeling and knowledge discovery for predictive rather than purely descriptive purposes.
Standard deviation	In statistics and probability theory, the standard deviation shows how much variation or dispersion from the average exists. A low standard deviation indicates that the data points tend to be very close to the mean (also called expected value); a high standard deviation indicates that the data points are spread out over a large range of values.
	The standard deviation of a random variable, statistical population, data set, or probability distribution is the square root of its variance.

4. Understanding and Comparing Distributions

Exponential smoothing	Exponential smoothing is a technique that can be applied to time series data, either to produce smoothed data for presentation, or to make forecasts. The time series data themselves are a sequence of observations. The observed phenomenon may be an essentially random process, or it may be an orderly, but noisy, process.
Moving average	In statistics, a moving average is a calculation to analyze data points by creating a series of averages of different subsets of the full data set. It is also called a moving mean (MM) or rolling mean and is a type of finite impulse response filter. Variations include: simple, and cumulative, or weighted forms (described below).

1. In statistics and probability theory, the _____ shows how much variation or dispersion from the average exists. A low _____ indicates that the data points tend to be very close to the mean (also called expected value); a high _____ indicates that the data points are spread out over a large range of values.

   The _____ of a random variable, statistical population, data set, or probability distribution is the square root of its variance.

   a. Barnardisation
   b. Collocation
   c. Standard deviation
   d. Crosstab

2. Analysis of data is a process of inspecting, cleaning, transforming, and modeling data with the goal of discovering useful information, suggesting conclusions, and supporting decision making. _____ has multiple facets and approaches, encompassing diverse techniques under a variety of names, in different business, science, and social science domains.

   Data mining is a particular _____ technique that focuses on modeling and knowledge discovery for predictive rather than purely descriptive purposes.

   a. Covariance
   b. Law of total covariance
   c. Law of total cumulance
   d. Data analysis

3. . _____ is a technique that can be applied to time series data, either to produce smoothed data for presentation, or to make forecasts. The time series data themselves are a sequence of observations.

The observed phenomenon may be an essentially random process, or it may be an orderly, but noisy, process.

a. Berlin procedure
b. Exponential smoothing
c. Cointegration
d. Convergent cross mapping

4. In statistics, a _____ is a calculation to analyze data points by creating a series of averages of different subsets of the full data set. It is also called a moving mean (MM) or rolling mean and is a type of finite impulse response filter. Variations include: simple, and cumulative, or weighted forms (described below).

a. Moving average
b. Chow test
c. Cointegration
d. Convergent cross mapping

5. _____ is the process of breaking a complex topic or substance into smaller parts to gain a better understanding of it. The technique has been applied in the study of mathematics and logic since before Aristotle (384-322 B.C)., though _____ as a formal concept is a relatively recent development.

The word comes from the Ancient Greek ?????s?? (analusis, 'a breaking up', from ana- 'up, throughout' and lysis 'a loosening').

a. Design science
b. Research
c. Survey research
d. Analysis

1. c
2. d
3. b
4. a
5. d

You can take the complete Chapter Practice Test

for 4. Understanding and Comparing Distributions
on all key terms, persons, places, and concepts.

Online 99 Cents

http://www.JustTheFacts101.com

Use www.JustTheFacts101.com for all your study needs

including Facts101's online interactive problem solving labs in

chemistry, statistics, mathematics, and more.

5. The Standard Deviation as a Ruler and the Normal Model

	Interquartile range
	Range
	Sampling
	Sampling distribution
	Correlation
	Standard deviation
	Statistic
	Condition
	Theorem
	Rounding

CHAPTER HIGHLIGHTS & NOTES: KEY TERMS, PEOPLE, PLACES, CONCEPTS

| Interquartile range | In statistics, the interdecile range is the difference between the first and the ninth deciles . The interdecile range is a measure of statistical dispersion of the values in a set of data, similar to the range and the interquartile range, and can be computed from the (non-parametric) seven-number summary.

Despite its simplicity, for estimating the standard deviation of a normal distribution, the scaled interdecile range gives a reasonably efficient estimator. |
|---|---|
| Range | In arithmetic, the range of a set of data is the difference between the largest and smallest values.

However, in descriptive statistics, this concept of range has a more complex meaning. The range is the size of the smallest interval which contains all the data and provides an indication of statistical dispersion. |

5. The Standard Deviation as a Ruler and the Normal Model

Sampling	In statistics, quality assurance, & survey methodology, sampling is concerned with the selection of a subset of individuals from within a statistical population to estimate characteristics of the whole population. Each observation measures one or more properties (such as weight, location, color) of observable bodies distinguished as independent objects or individuals. In survey sampling, weights can be applied to the data to adjust for the sample design, particularly stratified sampling.
Sampling distribution	In statistics, a sampling distribution or finite-sample distribution is the probability distribution of a given statistic based on a random sample. Sampling distributions are important in statistics because they provide a major simplification on the route to statistical inference. More specifically, they allow analytical considerations to be based on the sampling distribution of a statistic, rather than on the joint probability distribution of all the individual sample values.
Correlation	In statistics, dependence is any statistical relationship between two random variables or two sets of data. Correlation refers to any of a broad class of statistical relationships involving dependence. Familiar examples of dependent phenomena include the correlation between the physical statures of parents and their offspring, and the correlation between the demand for a product and its price.
Standard deviation	In statistics and probability theory, the standard deviation shows how much variation or dispersion from the average exists. A low standard deviation indicates that the data points tend to be very close to the mean (also called expected value); a high standard deviation indicates that the data points are spread out over a large range of values. The standard deviation of a random variable, statistical population, data set, or probability distribution is the square root of its variance.
Statistic	A statistic is a single measure of some attribute of a sample (e.g., its arithmetic mean value). It is calculated by applying a function (statistical algorithm) to the values of the items of the sample, which are known together as a set of data. More formally, statistical theory defines a statistic as a function of a sample where the function itself is independent of the sample's distribution; that is, the function can be stated before realization of the data.
Condition	Comprehensive treatment of the word 'condition' requires emphasizing that it is ambiguous in the sense of having multiple normal meanings and that its meanings are often vague in the sense of admitting borderline cases. According to the 2007 American Philosophy: an Encyclopedia, in one widely used sense, conditions are or resemble qualities, properties, features, characteristics, or attributes.

5. The Standard Deviation as a Ruler and the Normal Model

Theorem	In mathematics, a theorem is a statement that has been proven on the basis of previously established statements, such as other theorems--and generally accepted statements, such as axioms. The proof of a mathematical theorem is a logical argument for the theorem statement given in accord with the rules of a deductive system. The proof of a theorem is often interpreted as justification of the truth of the theorem statement.
Rounding	Rounding a numerical value means replacing it by another value that is approximately equal but has a shorter, simpler, or more explicit representation; for example, replacing £23.4476 with £23.45, or the fraction 312/937 with 1/3, or the expression √2 with 1.414.
	Rounding is often done on purpose to obtain a value that is easier to write and handle than the original. It may be done also to indicate the accuracy of a computed number; for example, a quantity that was computed as 123,456 but is known to be accurate only to within a few hundred units is better stated as 'about 123,500.'
	On the other hand, rounding introduces some round-off error in the result.

1. In statistics, the interdecile range is the difference between the first and the ninth deciles . The interdecile range is a measure of statistical dispersion of the values in a set of data, similar to the range and the _____ , and can be computed from the (non-parametric) seven-number summary.

    Despite its simplicity, for estimating the standard deviation of a normal distribution, the scaled interdecile range gives a reasonably efficient estimator.

    a. Interquartile range
    b. Mean
    c. Harmonic mean
    d. Weighted arithmetic mean

2. . In statistics, dependence is any statistical relationship between two random variables or two sets of data. _____ refers to any of a broad class of statistical relationships involving dependence.

    Familiar examples of dependent phenomena include the _____ between the physical statures of parents and their offspring, and the _____ between the demand for a product and its price.

    a. Correlation

b. Bagnold number

c. Beale number

d. Blake number

3. In arithmetic, the _____ of a set of data is the difference between the largest and smallest values.

However, in descriptive statistics, this concept of _____ has a more complex meaning. The _____ is the size of the smallest interval which contains all the data and provides an indication of statistical dispersion.

a. Range

b. Covariance

c. Law of total covariance

d. Law of total cumulance

4. In mathematics, a _____ is a statement that has been proven on the basis of previously established statements, such as other _____s--and generally accepted statements, such as axioms. The proof of a mathematical _____ is a logical argument for the _____ statement given in accord with the rules of a deductive system. The proof of a _____ is often interpreted as justification of the truth of the _____ statement.

a. Polish notation

b. Theorem

c. Propositional function

d. Rule of inference

5. In statistics, quality assurance, & survey methodology, _____ is concerned with the selection of a subset of individuals from within a statistical population to estimate characteristics of the whole population. Each observation measures one or more properties (such as weight, location, color) of observable bodies distinguished as independent objects or individuals. In survey _____, weights can be applied to the data to adjust for the sample design, particularly stratified _____.

a. Covariance

b. Law of total covariance

c. Law of total cumulance

d. Sampling

1. a
2. a
3. a
4. b
5. d

You can take the complete Chapter Practice Test

for 5. The Standard Deviation as a Ruler and the Normal Model
on all key terms, persons, places, and concepts.

Online 99 Cents

http://www.JustTheFacts101.com

Use www.JustTheFacts101.com for all your study needs

including Facts101's online interactive problem solving labs in

chemistry, statistics, mathematics, and more.

6. Scatterplots, Association, and Correlation

CHAPTER OUTLINE: KEY TERMS, PEOPLE, PLACES, CONCEPTS

_____	Association
_____	Correlation
_____	Direction
_____	Sample
_____	Line
_____	Independence
_____	Condition
_____	Newton
_____	Prediction
_____	Prediction interval
_____	Variable
_____	Deviation
_____	Standard deviation
_____	Coefficient
_____	Outlier
_____	Placebo effect

Association	In statistics, an association is any relationship between two measured quantities that renders them statistically dependent. The term 'association' is closely related to the term 'correlation.' Both terms imply that two or more variables vary according to some pattern. However, correlation is more rigidly defined by some correlation coefficient which measures the degree to which the association of the variables tends to a certain pattern.
Correlation	In statistics, dependence is any statistical relationship between two random variables or two sets of data. Correlation refers to any of a broad class of statistical relationships involving dependence. Familiar examples of dependent phenomena include the correlation between the physical statures of parents and their offspring, and the correlation between the demand for a product and its price.
Direction	Direction is the information contained in the relative position of one point with respect to another point without the distance information. Directions may be either relative to some indicated reference (the violins in a full orchestra are typically seated to the left of the conductor), or absolute according to some previously agreed upon frame of reference (New York City lies due west of Madrid). Direction is often indicated manually by an extended index finger or written as an arrow.
Sample	In statistics and quantitative research methodology, a data sample is a set of data collected and/or selected from a statistical population by a defined procedure.
Line	The line is a unit of measurement, one line being equal to $1/12$ of an English inch. It was defined as one-quarter of a barleycorn, which defined the inch even before 1066. The French (prior to 1799) ligne was similarly defined as $1/12$ of the pouce (meaning 'thumb', about an inch). Since the French pouce or inch was about 6% longer than the English inch, the 'line' was similarly longer.
Independence	In probability theory, to say that two events are independent means that the occurrence of one does not affect the probability of the other. Similarly, two random variables are independent if the realization of one does not affect the probability distribution of the other. The concept of independence extends to dealing with collections of more than two events or random variables.
Condition	Comprehensive treatment of the word 'condition' requires emphasizing that it is ambiguous in the sense of having multiple normal meanings and that its meanings are often vague in the sense of admitting borderline cases. According to the 2007 American Philosophy: an Encyclopedia, in one widely used sense, conditions are or resemble qualities, properties, features, characteristics, or attributes. In these senses, a condition is often denoted by a nominalization of a grammatical predicate: 'being equilateral' is a nominalization of the predicate 'is equilateral'.

6. Scatterplots, Association, and Correlation

Newton

Newton is a monotype by the English poet, painter and printmaker William Blake first completed in 1795, but reworked and reprinted in 1805. It is one of the 12 'Large Colour Prints' or 'Large Colour Printed Drawings' created between 1795 and 1805, which also include his series of images on the biblical ruler Nebuchadnezzar.

Isaac Newton is shown sitting naked and crouched on a rocky outcropping covered with algae, apparently at the bottom of the sea. His attention is focused upon diagrams he draws with a compass upon a scroll that appears to unravel from his mouth.

Prediction

A prediction or forecast is a statement about the way things will happen in the future, often but not always based on experience or knowledge. While there is much overlap between prediction and forecast, a prediction may be a statement that some outcome is expected, while a forecast is more specific, and may cover a range of possible outcomes.

Although guaranteed information about the future is in many cases impossible, prediction is necessary to allow plans to be made about possible developments; Howard H. Stevenson writes that prediction in business '... is at least two things: Important and hard.'

Prediction interval

In statistical inference, specifically predictive inference, a prediction interval is an estimate of an interval in which future observations will fall, with a certain probability, given what has already been observed. Prediction intervals are often used in regression analysis.

Prediction intervals are used in both frequentist statistics and Bayesian statistics: a prediction interval bears the same relationship to a future observation that a frequentist confidence interval or Bayesian credible interval bears to an unobservable population parameter: prediction intervals predict the distribution of individual future points, whereas confidence intervals and credible intervals of parameters predict the distribution of estimates of the true population mean or other quantity of interest that cannot be observed.

Variable

In elementary mathematics, a variable is an alphabetic character representing a number which is either arbitrary or not fully specified or unknown. Making algebraic computations with variables as if they were explicit numbers allows one to solve a range of problems in a single computation. A typical example is the quadratic formula, which allows to solve every quadratic equation by simply substituting the numeric values of the coefficients of the given equation to the variables that represent them.

Deviation

In mathematics and statistics, deviation is a measure of difference between the observed value of a variable and some other value, often that variable's mean. The sign of the deviation reports the direction of that difference (the deviation is positive when the observed value exceeds the reference value). The magnitude of the value indicates the size of the difference.

6. Scatterplots, Association, and Correlation

Standard deviation	In statistics and probability theory, the standard deviation shows how much variation or dispersion from the average exists. A low standard deviation indicates that the data points tend to be very close to the mean (also called expected value); a high standard deviation indicates that the data points are spread out over a large range of values.
	The standard deviation of a random variable, statistical population, data set, or probability distribution is the square root of its variance.
Coefficient	In mathematics, a coefficient is a multiplicative factor in some term of a polynomial, a series or any expression; it is usually a number, but in any case does not involve any variables of the expression. For instance in $7x^2 - 3xy + 1.5 + y$
	the first two terms respectively have the coefficients 7 and -3. The third term 1.5 is a constant. The final term does not have any explicitly written coefficient, but is considered to have coefficient 1, since multiplying by that factor would not change the term.
Outlier	In statistics, an outlier is an observation point that is distant from other observations. An outlier may be due to variability in the measurement or it may indicate experimental error; the latter are sometimes excluded from the data set.
	Outliers can occur by chance in any distribution, but they are often indicative either of measurement error or that the population has a heavy-tailed distribution.
Placebo effect	A placebo is a simulated or otherwise medically ineffectual treatment for a disease or other medical condition intended to deceive the recipient. Sometimes patients given a placebo treatment will have a perceived or actual improvement in a medical condition, a phenomenon commonly called the placebo effect.
	In medical research, placebos are given as control treatments and depend on the use of measured deception.

6. Scatterplots, Association, and Correlation

1. In statistics, an _____ is any relationship between two measured quantities that renders them statistically dependent. The term '_____' is closely related to the term 'correlation.' Both terms imply that two or more variables vary according to some pattern. However, correlation is more rigidly defined by some correlation coefficient which measures the degree to which the _____ of the variables tends to a certain pattern.

   a. Association
   b. Law of total covariance
   c. Law of total cumulance
   d. Law of total expectation

2. In statistics, dependence is any statistical relationship between two random variables or two sets of data. _____ refers to any of a broad class of statistical relationships involving dependence.

   Familiar examples of dependent phenomena include the _____ between the physical statures of parents and their offspring, and the _____ between the demand for a product and its price.

   a. Correlation
   b. Bagnold number
   c. Beale number
   d. Blake number

3. _____ is the information contained in the relative position of one point with respect to another point without the distance information. _____s may be either relative to some indicated reference (the violins in a full orchestra are typically seated to the left of the conductor), or absolute according to some previously agreed upon frame of reference (New York City lies due west of Madrid). _____ is often indicated manually by an extended index finger or written as an arrow.

   a. Direction
   b. Bankoff circle
   c. Base
   d. Bicentric polygon

4. In statistics and quantitative research methodology, a data _____ is a set of data collected and/or selected from a statistical population by a defined procedure.

   a. Correct sampling
   b. Sample
   c. Judgment sample
   d. Lot quality assurance sampling

5. The _____ is a unit of measurement, one _____ being equal to $1/12$ of an English inch. It was defined as one -quarter of a barleycorn, which defined the inch even before 1066. The French (prior to 1799) ligne was similarly defined as $1/12$ of the pouce (meaning 'thumb', about an inch). Since the French pouce or inch was about 6% longer than the English inch, the '_____' was similarly longer.

a. Line
b. Bamboo
c. Batman
d. Buddam

1. a

2. a

3. a

4. b

5. a

7. Linear Regression

CHAPTER OUTLINE: KEY TERMS, PEOPLE, PLACES. CONCEPTS

_____ | Linear regression

_____ | Regression

_____ | Linear model

_____ | Power

_____ | Residual

_____ | Hypothesis

_____ | Hypothesis test

_____ | Least squares

_____ | Test

_____ | Coefficient

_____ | Line

_____ | Slope

_____ | Condition

_____ | Newton

_____ | Standard deviation

_____ | Deviation

_____ | Random variable

7. Linear Regression

Linear regression	In statistics, linear regression is an approach for modeling the relationship between a scalar dependent variable y and one or more explanatory variables denoted X. The case of one explanatory variable is called simple linear regression. For more than one explanatory variable, the process is called multiple linear regression. (This term should be distinguished from multivariate linear regression, where multiple correlated dependent variables are predicted, rather than a single scalar variable).
Regression	Regression in medicine is a characteristic of diseases to show lighter symptoms without completely disappearing. At a later point, symptoms may return. These symptoms are then called recidive.
Linear model	In statistics, the term linear model is used in different ways according to the context. The most common occurrence is in connection with regression models and the term is often taken as synonymous with linear regression model. However, the term is also used in time series analysis with a different meaning.
Power	In physics, power is the rate of doing work. It is equivalent to an amount of energy consumed per unit time. In the MKS system, the unit of power is the joule per second (J/s), known as the watt in honor of James Watt, the eighteenth-century developer of the steam engine.
Residual	Loosely speaking, a residual is the error in a result. To be precise, suppose we want to find x such that $f(x) = b.$ Given an approximation x_0 of x, the residual is $b - f(x_0)$ whereas the error is $x_0 - x.$ If we do not know x, we cannot compute the error but we can compute the residual.
Hypothesis	A hypothesis is a proposed explanation for a phenomenon. For a hypothesis to be a scientific hypothesis, the scientific method requires that one can test it. Scientists generally base scientific hypotheses on previous observations that cannot satisfactorily be explained with the available scientific theories.
Hypothesis test	A statistical hypothesis test is a method of statistical inference using data from a scientific study. In statistics, a result is called statistically significant if it has been predicted as unlikely to have occurred by chance alone, according to a pre-determined threshold probability, the significance level. The phrase 'test of significance' was coined by statistician Ronald Fisher.
Least squares	The method of least squares is a standard approach to the approximate solution of overdetermined systems, i.e., sets of equations in which there are more equations than unknowns.

'Least squares' means that the overall solution minimizes the sum of the squares of the errors made in the results of every single equation.

The most important application is in data fitting.

Test	A test or examination is an assessment intended to measure a test-taker's knowledge, skill, aptitude, physical fitness, or classification in many other topics . A test may be administered orally, on paper, on a computer, or in a confined area that requires a test taker to physically perform a set of skills. Tests vary in style, rigor and requirements.
Coefficient	In mathematics, a coefficient is a multiplicative factor in some term of a polynomial, a series or any expression; it is usually a number, but in any case does not involve any variables of the expression. For instance in $7x^2 - 3xy + 1.5 + y$ the first two terms respectively have the coefficients 7 and -3. The third term 1.5 is a constant. The final term does not have any explicitly written coefficient, but is considered to have coefficient 1, since multiplying by that factor would not change the term.
Line	The line is a unit of measurement, one line being equal to $1/12$ of an English inch. It was defined as one-quarter of a barleycorn, which defined the inch even before 1066. The French (prior to 1799) ligne was similarly defined as $1/12$ of the pouce (meaning 'thumb', about an inch). Since the French pouce or inch was about 6% longer than the English inch, the 'line' was similarly longer.
Slope	In mathematics, the slope or gradient of a line is a number that describes both the direction and the steepness of the line. Slope is often denoted by the letter m. •The direction of a line is either increasing, decreasing, horizontal or vertical.•A line is increasing if it goes up from left to right.
Condition	Comprehensive treatment of the word 'condition' requires emphasizing that it is ambiguous in the sense of having multiple normal meanings and that its meanings are often vague in the sense of admitting borderline cases. According to the 2007 American Philosophy: an Encyclopedia, in one widely used sense, conditions are or resemble qualities, properties, features, characteristics, or attributes. In these senses, a condition is often denoted by a nominalization of a grammatical predicate: 'being equilateral' is a nominalization of the predicate 'is equilateral'.
Newton	Newton is a monotype by the English poet, painter and printmaker William Blake first completed in 1795, but reworked and reprinted in 1805. It is one of the 12 'Large Colour Prints' or 'Large Colour Printed Drawings' created between 1795 and 1805, which also include his series of images on the biblical ruler Nebuchadnezzar.

7. Linear Regression

Isaac Newton is shown sitting naked and crouched on a rocky outcropping covered with algae, apparently at the bottom of the sea. His attention is focused upon diagrams he draws with a compass upon a scroll that appears to unravel from his mouth.

Standard deviation

In statistics and probability theory, the standard deviation shows how much variation or dispersion from the average exists. A low standard deviation indicates that the data points tend to be very close to the mean (also called expected value); a high standard deviation indicates that the data points are spread out over a large range of values.

The standard deviation of a random variable, statistical population, data set, or probability distribution is the square root of its variance.

Deviation

In mathematics and statistics, deviation is a measure of difference between the observed value of a variable and some other value, often that variable's mean. The sign of the deviation reports the direction of that difference (the deviation is positive when the observed value exceeds the reference value). The magnitude of the value indicates the size of the difference.

Random variable

In probability and statistics, a random variable, aleatory variable or stochastic variable is a variable whose value is subject to variations due to chance . A random variable can take on a set of possible different values (similarly to other mathematical variables), each with an associated probability (if discrete) or a probability density function (if continuous), in contrast to other mathematical variables.

A random variable's possible values might represent the possible outcomes of a yet-to-be-performed experiment, or the possible outcomes of a past experiment whose already-existing value is uncertain (for example, as a result of incomplete information or imprecise measurements).

7. Linear Regression

1. In statistics, _____ is an approach for modeling the relationship between a scalar dependent variable y and one or more explanatory variables denoted X. The case of one explanatory variable is called simple _____. For more than one explanatory variable, the process is called multiple _____. (This term should be distinguished from multivariate _____, where multiple correlated dependent variables are predicted, rather than a single scalar variable).

   a. Backcasting
   b. Best linear unbiased prediction
   c. Linear regression
   d. Confidence region

2. Loosely speaking, a _____ is the error in a result. To be precise, suppose we want to find x such that $f(x) = b$.

   Given an approximation x_0 of x, the _____ is $b - f(x_0)$

   whereas the error is $x_0 - x$.

   If we do not know x, we cannot compute the error but we can compute the _____.

   a. Basis function
   b. Bernstein polynomial
   c. Bi-directional delay line
   d. Residual

3. _____ in medicine is a characteristic of diseases to show lighter symptoms without completely disappearing. At a later point, symptoms may return. These symptoms are then called recidive.

   a. 1947 New York City smallpox outbreak
   b. 1993 Four Corners hantavirus outbreak
   c. Regression
   d. 2012 Middle East respiratory syndrome coronavirus outbreak

4. In mathematics, the _____ or gradient of a line is a number that describes both the direction and the steepness of the line. _____ is often denoted by the letter m. •The direction of a line is either increasing, decreasing, horizontal or vertical.•A line is increasing if it goes up from left to right.

   a. Cartesian coordinate system
   b. Slope
   c. Clock angle problem
   d. Cognitively Guided Instruction

5. . In statistics, the term _____ is used in different ways according to the context. The most common occurrence is in connection with regression models and the term is often taken as synonymous with linear regression model.

7. Linear Regression

However, the term is also used in time series analysis with a different meaning.

a. Distributed lag
b. Linear model
c. Law of total covariance
d. Law of total cumulance

1. c
2. d
3. c
4. b
5. b

8. Regression Wisdom

CHAPTER OUTLINE: KEY TERMS, PEOPLE, PLACES, CONCEPTS

Condition

Linear regression

Regression

Difference

Error

Standard error

Extrapolation

Leverage

Outlier

Slope

Linearity

Causation

Independence

8. Regression Wisdom

Condition	Comprehensive treatment of the word 'condition' requires emphasizing that it is ambiguous in the sense of having multiple normal meanings and that its meanings are often vague in the sense of admitting borderline cases. According to the 2007 American Philosophy: an Encyclopedia, in one widely used sense, conditions are or resemble qualities, properties, features, characteristics, or attributes. In these senses, a condition is often denoted by a nominalization of a grammatical predicate: 'being equilateral' is a nominalization of the predicate 'is equilateral'.
Linear regression	In statistics, linear regression is an approach for modeling the relationship between a scalar dependent variable y and one or more explanatory variables denoted X. The case of one explanatory variable is called simple linear regression. For more than one explanatory variable, the process is called multiple linear regression. (This term should be distinguished from multivariate linear regression, where multiple correlated dependent variables are predicted, rather than a single scalar variable).
Regression	Regression in medicine is a characteristic of diseases to show lighter symptoms without completely disappearing. At a later point, symptoms may return. These symptoms are then called recidive.
Difference	Difference is a key concept of philosophy, denoting the process or set of properties by which one entity is distinguished from another within a relational field or a given conceptual system. In the Western philosophical system, difference is traditionally viewed as being opposed to identity, following the Principles of Leibniz, and in particular his Law of the Identity of indiscernibles. In structuralist and poststructuralist accounts, however, difference is understood to be constitutive of both meaning and identity.
Error	The word error entails different meanings and usages relative to how it is conceptually applied. The concrete meaning of the Latin word 'error' is 'wandering' or 'straying'. Unlike an illusion, an error or a mistake can sometimes be dispelled through knowledge (knowing that one is looking at a mirage and not at real water does not make the mirage disappear).
Standard error	The standard error is the standard deviation of the sampling distribution of a statistic. The term may also be used to refer to an estimate of that standard deviation, derived from a particular sample used to compute the estimate. For example, the sample mean is the usual estimator of a population mean.
Extrapolation	In mathematics, extrapolation is the process of estimating, beyond the original observation range, the value of a variable on the basis of its relationship with another variable. It is similar to interpolation, which produces estimates between known observations, but extrapolation is subject to greater uncertainty and a higher risk of producing meaningless results.

8. Regression Wisdom

Leverage	In statistics, leverage is a term used in connection with regression analysis and, in particular, in analyses aimed at identifying those observations that are far away from corresponding average predictor values. Leverage points do not necessarily have a large effect on the outcome of fitting regression models. Leverage points are those observations, if any, made at extreme or outlying values of the independent variables such that the lack of neighboring observations means that the fitted regression model will pass close to that particular observation.
Outlier	In statistics, an outlier is an observation point that is distant from other observations. An outlier may be due to variability in the measurement or it may indicate experimental error; the latter are sometimes excluded from the data set. Outliers can occur by chance in any distribution, but they are often indicative either of measurement error or that the population has a heavy-tailed distribution.
Slope	In mathematics, the slope or gradient of a line is a number that describes both the direction and the steepness of the line. Slope is often denoted by the letter m. •The direction of a line is either increasing, decreasing, horizontal or vertical.•A line is increasing if it goes up from left to right.
Linearity	In common usage, linearity refers to a function or relationship which can be graphically represented as a straight line, as in two quantities that are directly proportional to each other, such as voltage and current in a simple DC circuit, or the mass and weight of an object. A crude but simple example of this concept can be observed in the volume control of an audio amplifier. While our ears may (roughly) perceive a relatively even gradation of volume as the control goes from 1 to 10, the electrical power consumed in the speaker is rising geometrically with each numerical increment.
Causation	Causation is the 'causal relationship between conduct and result'. That is to say that causation provides a means of connecting conduct with a resulting effect, typically an injury. In criminal law, it is defined as the actus reus (an action) from which the specific injury or other effect arose and is combined with mens rea (a state of mind) to comprise the elements of guilt.
Independence	In probability theory, to say that two events are independent means that the occurrence of one does not affect the probability of the other. Similarly, two random variables are independent if the realization of one does not affect the probability distribution of the other. The concept of independence extends to dealing with collections of more than two events or random variables.

8. Regression Wisdom

1. _____ in medicine is a characteristic of diseases to show lighter symptoms without completely disappearing. At a later point, symptoms may return. These symptoms are then called recidive.

   a. Regression
   b. 1993 Four Corners hantavirus outbreak
   c. 2003 Midwest monkeypox outbreak
   d. 2012 Middle East respiratory syndrome coronavirus outbreak

2. _____ is a key concept of philosophy, denoting the process or set of properties by which one entity is distinguished from another within a relational field or a given conceptual system. In the Western philosophical system, _____ is traditionally viewed as being opposed to identity, following the Principles of Leibniz, and in particular his Law of the Identity of indiscernibles. In structuralist and poststructuralist accounts, however, _____ is understood to be constitutive of both meaning and identity.

   a. Belief revision
   b. Difference
   c. Canon
   d. Ceqli

3. Comprehensive treatment of the word '_____' requires emphasizing that it is ambiguous in the sense of having multiple normal meanings and that its meanings are often vague in the sense of admitting borderline cases.

   According to the 2007 American Philosophy: an Encyclopedia, in one widely used sense, _____s are or resemble qualities, properties, features, characteristics, or attributes. In these senses, a _____ is often denoted by a nominalization of a grammatical predicate: 'being equilateral' is a nominalization of the predicate 'is equilateral'.

   a. Belief revision
   b. Condition
   c. Canon
   d. Ceqli

4. In statistics, _____ is an approach for modeling the relationship between a scalar dependent variable y and one or more explanatory variables denoted X. The case of one explanatory variable is called simple _____. For more than one explanatory variable, the process is called multiple _____. (This term should be distinguished from multivariate _____, where multiple correlated dependent variables are predicted, rather than a single scalar variable).

   a. Backcasting
   b. Linear regression
   c. Blind deconvolution
   d. Confidence region

5. . In mathematics, the _____ or gradient of a line is a number that describes both the direction and the steepness of the line. _____ is often denoted by the letter m.

•The direction of a line is either increasing, decreasing, horizontal or vertical.•A line is increasing if it goes up from left to right.

a. Cartesian coordinate system
b. Slope
c. Clock angle problem
d. Cognitively Guided Instruction

1. a
2. b
3. b
4. b
5. b

You can take the complete Chapter Practice Test

for 8. Regression Wisdom
on all key terms, persons, places, and concepts.

Online 99 Cents

http://www.JustTheFacts101.com

Use www.JustTheFacts101.com for all your study needs

including Facts101's online interactive problem solving labs in

chemistry, statistics, mathematics, and more.

9. Understanding Randomness

CHAPTER OUTLINE: KEY TERMS, PEOPLE, PLACES, CONCEPTS

	Randomness
	Simulation
	Randomization
	Independence
	Lottery
	Dice

CHAPTER HIGHLIGHTS & NOTES: KEY TERMS, PEOPLE, PLACES, CONCEPTS

Randomness	Randomness means lack of pattern or predictability in events. Randomness suggests a non-order or non-coherence in a sequence of symbols or steps, such that there is no intelligible pattern or combination. Applied usage in science, mathematics and statistics recognizes a lack of predictability when referring to randomness, but admits regularities in the occurrences of events whose outcomes are not certain.
Simulation	Simulation is the imitation of the operation of a real-world process or system over time. The act of simulating something first requires that a model be developed; this model represents the key characteristics or behaviors/functions of the selected physical or abstract system or process. The model represents the system itself, whereas the simulation represents the operation of the system over time.
Randomization	Randomization is the process of making something random; this means: Randomization is not haphazard. Instead, a random process is a sequence of random variables describing a process whose outcomes do not follow a deterministic pattern, but follow an evolution described by probability distributions. For example, a random sample of individuals from a population refers to a sample where every individual has a known probability of being sampled.
Independence	In probability theory, to say that two events are independent means that the occurrence of one does not affect the probability of the other.

9. Understanding Randomness

Similarly, two random variables are independent if the realization of one does not affect the probability distribution of the other.

The concept of independence extends to dealing with collections of more than two events or random variables.

Lottery

In expected utility theory, a lottery is a discrete distribution of probability on a set of states of nature. The elements of a lottery correspond to the probability that a certain outcome arises from a given state of nature. In economics, individuals are assumed to rank lotteries according to a rational system of preferences, although it is now accepted that people make irrational choices systematically.

Dice

Dice are small throwable objects with multiple resting positions, used for generating random numbers. Dice are suitable as gambling devices for games like craps, and are also used in non-gambling tabletop games.

A traditional die is a rounded cube, with each of its six faces showing a different number of dots (pips) from 1 to 6. When thrown or rolled, the die comes to rest showing on its upper surface a random integer from one to six, each value being equally likely.

1. _____ is the process of making something random; this means:

   _____ is not haphazard. Instead, a random process is a sequence of random variables describing a process whose outcomes do not follow a deterministic pattern, but follow an evolution described by probability distributions. For example, a random sample of individuals from a population refers to a sample where every individual has a known probability of being sampled.

   a. Determinism
   b. Global Consciousness Project
   c. Mendelian randomization
   d. Randomization

2. . _____ means lack of pattern or predictability in events. _____ suggests a non-order or non-coherence in a sequence of symbols or steps, such that there is no intelligible pattern or combination.

   Applied usage in science, mathematics and statistics recognizes a lack of predictability when referring to _____, but admits regularities in the occurrences of events whose outcomes are not certain.

  a. Randomness
  b. Biological warfare
  c. Questionable cause
  d. Causal inference

3. _____ is the imitation of the operation of a real-world process or system over time. The act of simulating something first requires that a model be developed; this model represents the key characteristics or behaviors/functions of the selected physical or abstract system or process. The model represents the system itself, whereas the _____ represents the operation of the system over time.

  a. Simulation
  b. Backtracking
  c. Bayesian search theory
  d. Berth allocation problem

4. In probability theory, to say that two events are independent means that the occurrence of one does not affect the probability of the other. Similarly, two random variables are independent if the realization of one does not affect the probability distribution of the other.

  The concept of _____ extends to dealing with collections of more than two events or random variables.

  a. Independence
  b. B-convex space
  c. Bean machine
  d. Chain rule

5. In expected utility theory, a _____ is a discrete distribution of probability on a set of states of nature. The elements of a _____ correspond to the probability that a certain outcome arises from a given state of nature. In economics, individuals are assumed to rank _____(ies) according to a rational system of preferences, although it is now accepted that people make irrational choices systematically.

  a. Lottery
  b. Classical general equilibrium model
  c. Constant elasticity of substitution
  d. Discounted utility

1. d
2. a
3. a
4. a
5. a

You can take the complete Chapter Practice Test

for 9. Understanding Randomness
on all key terms, persons, places, and concepts.

Online 99 Cents

http://www.JustTheFacts101.com

Use www.JustTheFacts101.com for all your study needs

including Facts101's online interactive problem solving labs in

chemistry, statistics, mathematics, and more.

10. Sample Surveys

Sample

Bias

Population

Marginal distribution

Matching

Randomization

Census

Sample size

Size

Statistic

Parameter

Population model

Simple random sample

Difference

Error

Regression

Standard error

Sampling error

Sampling frame

Sampling

Cluster sampling

CHAPTER OUTLINE: KEY TERMS, PEOPLE, PLACES, CONCEPTS

Pilot study

Response bias

Cluster

Experiment

Random assignment

Level

Blocking

Independence

Peirce

Replication

Complement

Statistical significance

Control

Double-blind

Placebo

Placebo effect

Value

Confounding

Distribution

10. Sample Surveys

Sample	In statistics and quantitative research methodology, a data sample is a set of data collected and/or selected from a statistical population by a defined procedure.
Bias	Bias is an inclination of temperament or outlook to present or hold a partial perspective and a refusal to even consider the possible merits of alternative points of view. People may be biased toward or against an individual, a race, a religion, a social class, or a political party. Biased means one-sided, lacking a neutral viewpoint, not having an open mind.
Population	A statistical population is a set of individuals or objects of interest. A subset of a population is called a subpopulation. If different subpopulations have different properties, so the overall population is heterogeneous, the properties and response of the overall population can often be better understood if it is first separated into distinct subpopulations. For instance, a particular medicine may have different effects on different subpopulations, and these effects may be obscured or dismissed if such special subpopulations are not identified and examined in isolation. Similarly, one can often estimate parameters more accurately if one separates out subpopulations: the distribution of heights among people is better modeled by considering men and women as separate subpopulations, for instance.
Marginal distribution	In probability theory and statistics, the marginal distribution of a subset of a collection of random variables is the probability distribution of the variables contained in the subset. It gives the probabilities of various values of the variables in the subset without reference to the values of the other variables. This contrasts with a conditional distribution, which gives the probabilities contingent upon the values of the other variables.
Matching	In the mathematical discipline of graph theory, a matching or independent edge set in a graph is a set of edges without common vertices. It may also be an entire graph consisting of edges without common vertices.
Randomization	Randomization is the process of making something random; this means: Randomization is not haphazard. Instead, a random process is a sequence of random variables describing a process whose outcomes do not follow a deterministic pattern, but follow an evolution described by probability distributions. For example, a random sample of individuals from a population refers to a sample where every individual has a known probability of being sampled.
Census	A census is the procedure of systematically acquiring and recording information about the members of a given population. It is a regularly occurring and official count of a particular population.

Sample size	Sample size determination is the act of choosing the number of observations or replicates to include in a statistical sample. The sample size is an important feature of any empirical study in which the goal is to make inferences about a population from a sample. In practice, the sample size used in a study is determined based on the expense of data collection, and the need to have sufficient statistical power.
Size	In statistics, the size of a statistical test is the maximum of the probabilities of a type I error, i.e. of the probabilities of falsely rejecting the null hypothesis. In the case of a simple null hypothesis the size is the only possible probability of a type I error. The size of a test is denoted by the Greek letter a (alpha).
Statistic	A statistic is a single measure of some attribute of a sample (e.g., its arithmetic mean value). It is calculated by applying a function (statistical algorithm) to the values of the items of the sample, which are known together as a set of data.
	More formally, statistical theory defines a statistic as a function of a sample where the function itself is independent of the sample's distribution; that is, the function can be stated before realization of the data.
Parameter	A parameter, in its common meaning, is a characteristic, feature, or measurable factor that can help in defining a particular system. A parameter is an important element to consider in evaluation or comprehension of an event, project, or situation. Parameter has more specific interpretations in mathematics, logic, linguistics, environmental science, and other disciplines.
Population model	A population model is a type of mathematical model that is applied to the study of population dynamics.
	Models allow a better understanding of how complex interactions and processes work. Modeling of dynamic interactions in nature can provide a manageable way of understanding how numbers change over time or in relation to each other.
Simple random sample	In statistics, a simple random sample is a subset of individuals chosen from a larger set (a population). Each individual is chosen randomly and entirely by chance, such that each individual has the same probability of being chosen at any stage during the sampling process, and each subset of k individuals has the same probability of being chosen for the sample as any other subset of k individuals. This process and technique is known as simple random sampling, and should not be confused with systematic random sampling.
Difference	Difference is a key concept of philosophy, denoting the process or set of properties by which one entity is distinguished from another within a relational field or a given conceptual system. In the Western philosophical system, difference is traditionally viewed as being opposed to identity, following the Principles of Leibniz, and in particular his Law of the Identity of indiscernibles.

10. Sample Surveys

Error	The word error entails different meanings and usages relative to how it is conceptually applied. The concrete meaning of the Latin word 'error' is 'wandering' or 'straying'. Unlike an illusion, an error or a mistake can sometimes be dispelled through knowledge (knowing that one is looking at a mirage and not at real water does not make the mirage disappear).
Regression	Regression in medicine is a characteristic of diseases to show lighter symptoms without completely disappearing. At a later point, symptoms may return. These symptoms are then called recidive.
Standard error	The standard error is the standard deviation of the sampling distribution of a statistic. The term may also be used to refer to an estimate of that standard deviation, derived from a particular sample used to compute the estimate. For example, the sample mean is the usual estimator of a population mean.
Sampling error	In statistics, sampling error is incurred when the statistical characteristics of a population are estimated from a subset, or sample, of that population. Since the sample does not include all members of the population, statistics on the sample, such as means and quantiles, generally differ from parameters on the entire population. For example, if one measures the height of a thousand individuals from a country of one million, the average height of the thousand is typically not the same as the average height of all one million people in the country.
Sampling frame	In statistics, a sampling frame is the source material or device from which a sample is drawn. It is a list of all those within a population who can be sampled, and may include individuals, households or institutions. Importance of the sampling frame is stressed by Jessen:' In many practical situations the frame is a matter of choice to the survey planner, and sometimes a critical one.'
Sampling	In statistics, quality assurance, & survey methodology, sampling is concerned with the selection of a subset of individuals from within a statistical population to estimate characteristics of the whole population. Each observation measures one or more properties (such as weight, location, color) of observable bodies distinguished as independent objects or individuals. In survey sampling, weights can be applied to the data to adjust for the sample design, particularly stratified sampling.
Cluster sampling	Cluster sampling is a sampling technique used when 'natural' but relatively homogeneous groupings are evident in a statistical population. It is often used in marketing research. In this technique, the total population is divided into these groups (or clusters) and a simple random sample of the groups is selected.

10. Sample Surveys

Pilot study	A pilot experiment, also called a pilot study, is a small scale preliminary study conducted in order to evaluate feasibility, time, cost, adverse events, and effect size in an attempt to predict an appropriate sample size and improve upon the study design prior to performance of a full-scale research project. Pilot studies, therefore, may not be appropriate for case studies.
Response bias	Response bias is a type of cognitive bias which can affect the results of a statistical survey if respondents answer questions in the way they think the questioner wants them to answer rather than according to their true beliefs. This may occur if the questioner is obviously angling for a particular answer (as in push polling) or if the respondent wishes to please the questioner by answering what appears to be the 'morally right' answer. An example of the latter might be if a woman surveys a man on his attitudes to domestic violence, or someone who obviously cares about the environment asks people how much they value a wilderness area.
Cluster	Clinical trials units are specialised biomedical research units which design, centrally coordinate and analyse clinical trials and other studies. Some CTUs specialise in different methodologies, such as randomised controlled trials, cluster randomised trials, surgical trials, and health services research. Some specialise in one disease type, whereas others are generic units.
Experiment	An experiment is an orderly procedure carried out with the goal of verifying, refuting, or establishing the validity of a hypothesis. Controlled experiments provide insight into cause-and-effect by demonstrating what outcome occurs when a particular factor is manipulated. Controlled experiments vary greatly in their goal and scale, but always rely on repeatable procedure and logical analysis of the results.
Random assignment	Random assignment or random placement is an experimental technique for assigning subjects to different treatments . The thinking behind random assignment is that by randomizing treatment assignment, then the group attributes for the different treatments will be roughly equivalent and therefore any effect observed between treatment groups can be linked to the treatment effect and is not a characteristic of the individuals in the group. In experimental design, random assignment of participants in experiments or treatment and control groups help to ensure that any differences between and within the groups are not systematic at the outset of the experiment.
Level	In the International System of Quantities, a level is the logarithm of the ratio of a quantity Q to a reference value of that quantity, Q_0. Examples are sound pressure level, sound power level and sound exposure level. In equation form: $L_Q = \log(Q/Q_0)$.
Blocking	In the statistical theory of the design of experiments, blocking is the arranging of experimental units in groups that are similar to one another. For example, an experiment is designed to test a new drug on patients.

10. Sample Surveys

Independence	In probability theory, to say that two events are independent means that the occurrence of one does not affect the probability of the other. Similarly, two random variables are independent if the realization of one does not affect the probability distribution of the other. The concept of independence extends to dealing with collections of more than two events or random variables.
Peirce	Peirce is a surname. It may refer to some notable people with this surname:
Replication	In engineering, science, and statistics, replication is the repetition of an experimental condition so that the variability associated with the phenomenon can be estimated. ASTM, in standard E1847, defines replication as 'the repetition of the set of all the treatment combinations to be compared in an experiment. Each of the repetitions is called a replicate.' Replication is not the same as repeated measurements of the same item: they are dealt with differently in statistical experimental design and data analysis.
Complement	In set theory, a complement of a set A refers to things not in A. The relative complement of A with respect to a set B is the set of elements in B but not in A. When all sets under consideration are considered to be subsets of a given set U, the absolute complement of A is the set of all elements in U but not in A.
Statistical significance	Statistical significance is the probability that an effect is not due to just chance alone. It is an integral part of statistical hypothesis testing where it is used as an important value judgment. In statistics, a result is considered significant not because it is important or meaningful, but because it has been predicted as unlikely to have occurred by chance alone.
Control	Controlling is one of the managerial functions like planning, organizing, staffing and directing. It is an important function because it helps to check the errors and to take the corrective action so that deviation from standards are minimized and stated goals of the organization are achieved in a desired manner. According to modern concepts, control is a foreseeing action whereas earlier concept of control was used only when errors were detected.
Double-blind	A blind or blinded experiment is an experiment in which information about the test that might lead to bias in the results is concealed from the tester, the subject, or both until after the test. Bias may be intentional or unconscious. If both tester and subject are blinded, the trial is a double-blind trial.
Placebo	A placebo is a simulated or otherwise medically ineffectual treatment for a disease or other medical condition intended to deceive the recipient.

Sometimes patients given a placebo treatment will have a perceived or actual improvement in a medical condition, a phenomenon commonly called the placebo effect.

In medical research, placebos are given as control treatments and depend on the use of measured deception.

Placebo effect	A placebo is a simulated or otherwise medically ineffectual treatment for a disease or other medical condition intended to deceive the recipient. Sometimes patients given a placebo treatment will have a perceived or actual improvement in a medical condition, a phenomenon commonly called the placebo effect.

In medical research, placebos are given as control treatments and depend on the use of measured deception. |
| Value | In ethics, value denotes something's degree of importance, with the aim of determining what action or life is best to do or live, or at least attempt to describe the value of different actions (Axiology). It may be described as treating actions themselves as abstract objects, putting value to them. It deals with right conduct and good life, in the sense that a highly, or at least relatively highly, valuable action may be regarded as ethically 'good' (adjective sense), and an action of low, or at least relatively low, value may be regarded as 'bad'. |
| Confounding | In statistics, a confounding variable (also confounding factor, a confound, or confounder) is an extraneous variable in a statistical model that correlates with both the dependent variable and the independent variable. A perceived relationship between an independent variable and a dependent variable that has been misestimated due to the failure to account for a confounding factor is termed a spurious relationship, and the presence of misestimation for this reason is termed omitted-variable bias. In the case of risk assessments evaluating the magnitude and nature of risk to human health, it is important to control for confounding to isolate the effect of a particular hazard such as a food additive, pesticide, or new drug. |
| Distribution | In algebra and number theory, a distribution is a function on a system of finite sets into an abelian group which is analogous to an integral: it is thus the algebraic analogue of a distribution in the sense of generalised function.

The original examples of distributions occur, unnamed, as functions f on Q/Z
$$\text{satisfying } \sum_{r=0}^{N-1} \phi\left(x + \frac{r}{N}\right) = \phi(Nx) \ .$$

We shall call these ordinary distributions. They also occur in p-adic integration theory in Iwasawa theory. |

10. Sample Surveys

1. _____ is a sampling technique used when 'natural' but relatively homogeneous groupings are evident in a statistical population. It is often used in marketing research. In this technique, the total population is divided into these groups (or clusters) and a simple random sample of the groups is selected.

   a. Cluster sampling
   b. Law of total covariance
   c. Law of total cumulance
   d. Law of total expectation

2. _____ is an inclination of temperament or outlook to present or hold a partial perspective and a refusal to even consider the possible merits of alternative points of view. People may be biased toward or against an individual, a race, a religion, a social class, or a political party. Biased means one-sided, lacking a neutral viewpoint, not having an open mind.

   a. Covariance
   b. Bias
   c. Law of total cumulance
   d. Law of total expectation

3. A _____, in its common meaning, is a characteristic, feature, or measurable factor that can help in defining a particular system. A _____ is an important element to consider in evaluation or comprehension of an event, project, or situation. _____ has more specific interpretations in mathematics, logic, linguistics, environmental science, and other disciplines.

   a. Parameter
   b. L-statistic
   c. Parameter space
   d. Pivotal quantity

4. A _____ is a single measure of some attribute of a sample (e.g., its arithmetic mean value). It is calculated by applying a function (statistical algorithm) to the values of the items of the sample, which are known together as a set of data.

   More formally, statistical theory defines a _____ as a function of a sample where the function itself is independent of the sample's distribution; that is, the function can be stated before realization of the data.

   a. Statistic
   b. L-statistic
   c. Parameter space
   d. Pivotal quantity

5. . In statistics and quantitative research methodology, a data _____ is a set of data collected and/or selected from a statistical population by a defined procedure.

   a. Correct sampling
   b. Deep sampling
   c. Sample

1. a
2. b
3. a
4. a
5. c

You can take the complete Chapter Practice Test

for 10. Sample Surveys
on all key terms, persons, places, and concepts.

Online 99 Cents

http://www.JustTheFacts101.com

Use www.JustTheFacts101.com for all your study needs

including Facts101's online interactive problem solving labs in

chemistry, statistics, mathematics, and more.

11. From Randomness to Probability

CHAPTER OUTLINE: KEY TERMS, PEOPLE, PLACES, CONCEPTS

	Probability
	Sample space
	Independence
	Law of averages
	Law of large numbers
	Multiplication
	Complement
	Empirical
	Large numbers

CHAPTER HIGHLIGHTS & NOTES: KEY TERMS, PEOPLE, PLACES, CONCEPTS

Probability

Probability is a measure of the likeliness that an event will occur.

Probability is used to quantify an attitude of mind towards some proposition of whose truth we are not certain. The proposition of interest is usually of the form 'Will a specific event occur?' The attitude of mind is of the form 'How certain are we that the event will occur?' The certainty we adopt can be described in terms of a numerical measure and this number, between 0 and 1 (where 0 indicates impossibility and 1 indicates certainty), we call probability.

Sample space

In probability theory, the sample space of an experiment or random trial is the set of all possible outcomes or results of that experiment. A sample space is usually denoted using set notation, and the possible outcomes are listed as elements in the set. It is common to refer to a sample space by the labels S, O, or U (for 'universal set').

Independence

In probability theory, to say that two events are independent means that the occurrence of one does not affect the probability of the other. Similarly, two random variables are independent if the realization of one does not affect the probability distribution of the other.

11. From Randomness to Probability

Law of averages	The law of averages is a layman's term used to express a belief that outcomes of a random event will 'even out' within a small sample. As invoked in everyday life, the 'law' usually reflects bad statistics or wishful thinking rather than any mathematical principle. While there is a real theorem that a random variable will reflect its underlying probability over a very large sample, the law of averages typically assumes that unnatural short-term 'balance' must occur.
Law of large numbers	In probability theory, the law of large numbers is a theorem that describes the result of performing the same experiment a large number of times. According to the law, the average of the results obtained from a large number of trials should be close to the expected value, and will tend to become closer as more trials are performed. The LLN is important because it 'guarantees' stable long-term results for the averages of random events.
Multiplication	Multiplication is the third basic mathematical operation of arithmetic, the others being addition, subtraction and division (the division is the fourth one, because it requires multiplication to be defined). The multiplication of two whole numbers is equivalent to the addition of one of them with itself as many times as the value of the other one; for example, 3 multiplied by 4 (often said as '3 times 4') can be calculated by adding 4 copies of 3 together: $3 \times 4 = 3 + 3 + 3 + 3 = 12$ Here 3 and 4 are the 'factors' and 12 is the 'product'. One of the main properties of multiplication is that the result does not depend on the place of the factor that is repeatedly added to itself (commutative property).
Complement	In set theory, a complement of a set A refers to things not in A. The relative complement of A with respect to a set B is the set of elements in B but not in A. When all sets under consideration are considered to be subsets of a given set U, the absolute complement of A is the set of all elements in U but not in A.
Empirical	Empirical evidence (also empirical data, sense experience, empirical knowledge, or the a posteriori) is a source of knowledge acquired by means of observation or experimentation. The term comes from the Greek word for experience, ?μpe???a (empeiría). Empirical evidence is information that justifies a belief in the truth or falsity of an empirical claim.
Large numbers	Very large numbers often occur in fields such as mathematics, cosmology, cryptography, and statistical mechanics. Sometimes people refer to numbers as being 'astronomically large'.

11. From Randomness to Probability

1. In probability theory, the _____ is a theorem that describes the result of performing the same experiment a large number of times. According to the law, the average of the results obtained from a large number of trials should be close to the expected value, and will tend to become closer as more trials are performed.

   The LLN is important because it 'guarantees' stable long-term results for the averages of random events.

   a. Bussgang theorem
   b. Continuous mapping theorem
   c. Law of large numbers
   d. Dominated convergence theorem

2. In probability theory, to say that two events are independent means that the occurrence of one does not affect the probability of the other. Similarly, two random variables are independent if the realization of one does not affect the probability distribution of the other.

   The concept of _____ extends to dealing with collections of more than two events or random variables.

   a. Independence
   b. B-convex space
   c. Bean machine
   d. Chain rule

3. _____ is a measure of the likeliness that an event will occur.

   _____ is used to quantify an attitude of mind towards some proposition of whose truth we are not certain. The proposition of interest is usually of the form 'Will a specific event occur?' The attitude of mind is of the form 'How certain are we that the event will occur?' The certainty we adopt can be described in terms of a numerical measure and this number, between 0 and 1 (where 0 indicates impossibility and 1 indicates certainty), we call _____.

   a. Concomitant
   b. Marginal structural model
   c. Probability
   d. Design science

4. In probability theory, the _____ of an experiment or random trial is the set of all possible outcomes or results of that experiment. A _____ is usually denoted using set notation, and the possible outcomes are listed as elements in the set. It is common to refer to a _____ by the labels S, O, or U (for 'universal set').

   a. Bayesian programming
   b. Sample space
   c. Bean machine
   d. Chain rule

5. In set theory, a _____ of a set A refers to things not in A. The relative _____ of A with respect to a set B is the set of elements in B but not in A. When all sets under consideration are considered to be subsets of a given set U, the absolute _____ of A is the set of all elements in U but not in A.

   a. Band sum
   b. Binary operation
   c. Complement
   d. Cap product

1. c
2. a
3. c
4. b
5. c

You can take the complete Chapter Practice Test

for 11. From Randomness to Probability
on all key terms, persons, places, and concepts.

Online 99 Cents

http://www.JustTheFacts101.com

Use www.JustTheFacts101.com for all your study needs

including Facts101's online interactive problem solving labs in

chemistry, statistics, mathematics, and more.

12. Probability Rules!

CHAPTER OUTLINE: KEY TERMS, PEOPLE, PLACES. CONCEPTS

	Conditional probability
	Probability
	Conditional distribution
	Distribution
	Independence
	Chi-square test
	Test

CHAPTER HIGHLIGHTS & NOTES: KEY TERMS, PEOPLE, PLACES, CONCEPTS

Conditional probability	In probability theory, a conditional probability measures the probability of an event given that another event has occurred. If the events are A and B respectively, this is said to be 'the probability of A given B'. It is commonly denoted by $P(A\backslash B)$, or sometimes $P_B(A)$.
Probability	Probability is a measure of the likeliness that an event will occur. Probability is used to quantify an attitude of mind towards some proposition of whose truth we are not certain. The proposition of interest is usually of the form 'Will a specific event occur?' The attitude of mind is of the form 'How certain are we that the event will occur?' The certainty we adopt can be described in terms of a numerical measure and this number, between 0 and 1 (where 0 indicates impossibility and 1 indicates certainty), we call probability.
Conditional distribution	In probability theory and statistics, given two jointly distributed random variables X and Y, the conditional probability distribution of Y given X is the probability distribution of Y when X is known to be a particular value; in some cases the conditional probabilities may be expressed as functions containing the unspecified value x of X as a parameter. In case that both 'X' and 'Y' are categorical variables, conditional probability table is typically used to represent the conditional probability. The conditional distribution contrasts with the marginal distribution of a random variable, which is its distribution without reference to the value of the other variable.

12. Probability Rules!

Distribution	In algebra and number theory, a distribution is a function on a system of finite sets into an abelian group which is analogous to an integral: it is thus the algebraic analogue of a distribution in the sense of generalised function.

The original examples of distributions occur, unnamed, as functions f on Q/Z

satisfying $$\sum_{r=0}^{N-1} \phi\left(x + \frac{r}{N}\right) = \phi(Nx) \ .$$

We shall call these ordinary distributions. They also occur in p-adic integration theory in Iwasawa theory. |
| Independence | In probability theory, to say that two events are independent means that the occurrence of one does not affect the probability of the other. Similarly, two random variables are independent if the realization of one does not affect the probability distribution of the other.

The concept of independence extends to dealing with collections of more than two events or random variables. |
| Chi-square test | A chi-squared test, also referred to as chi-square test or χ^2 test, is any statistical hypothesis test in which the sampling distribution of the test statistic is a chi-squared distribution when the null hypothesis is true. Also considered a chi-squared test is a test in which this is asymptotically true, meaning that the sampling distribution (if the null hypothesis is true) can be made to approximate a chi-squared distribution as closely as desired by making the sample size large enough.

Some examples of chi-squared tests where the chi-squared distribution is only approximately valid:•Pearson's chi-squared test, also known as the chi-squared goodness-of-fit test or chi-squared test for independence. |
| Test | A test or examination is an assessment intended to measure a test-taker's knowledge, skill, aptitude, physical fitness, or classification in many other topics . A test may be administered orally, on paper, on a computer, or in a confined area that requires a test taker to physically perform a set of skills. Tests vary in style, rigor and requirements. |

12. Probability Rules!

1. In probability theory, a _____ measures the probability of an event given that another event has occurred. If the events are A and B respectively, this is said to be 'the probability of A given B'. It is commonly denoted by P(A\B), or sometimes $P_B(A)$.

    a. Bayesian programming
    b. B-convex space
    c. Conditional probability
    d. Chain rule

2. _____ is a measure of the likeliness that an event will occur.

    _____ is used to quantify an attitude of mind towards some proposition of whose truth we are not certain. The proposition of interest is usually of the form 'Will a specific event occur?' The attitude of mind is of the form 'How certain are we that the event will occur?' The certainty we adopt can be described in terms of a numerical measure and this number, between 0 and 1 (where 0 indicates impossibility and 1 indicates certainty), we call _____.

    a. Concomitant
    b. Probability
    c. Research
    d. Design science

3. In probability theory and statistics, given two jointly distributed random variables X and Y, the conditional probability distribution of Y given X is the probability distribution of Y when X is known to be a particular value; in some cases the conditional probabilities may be expressed as functions containing the unspecified value x of X as a parameter. In case that both 'X' and 'Y' are categorical variables, conditional probability table is typically used to represent the conditional probability. The _____ contrasts with the marginal distribution of a random variable, which is its distribution without reference to the value of the other variable.

    a. 2-EPT probability density function
    b. Manhattan Project
    c. Conditional distribution
    d. Design science

4.. In algebra and number theory, a _____ is a function on a system of finite sets into an abelian group which is analogous to an integral: it is thus the algebraic analogue of a _____ in the sense of generalised function.

    The original examples of _____s occur, unnamed, as functions f on Q/Z

    $$\text{satisfying } \sum_{r=0}^{N-1} \phi\left(x + \frac{r}{N}\right) = \phi(Nx) .$$

    We shall call these ordinary _____s. They also occur in p-adic integration theory in Iwasawa theory.

a. Binomial
b. Canonical form
c. Closed-form expression
d. Distribution

5. In probability theory, to say that two events are independent means that the occurrence of one does not affect the probability of the other. Similarly, two random variables are independent if the realization of one does not affect the probability distribution of the other.

The concept of _____ extends to dealing with collections of more than two events or random variables.

a. Bayesian programming
b. B-convex space
c. Independence
d. Chain rule

1. c

2. b

3. c

4. d

5. c

You can take the complete Chapter Practice Test

for 12. Probability Rules!
on all key terms, persons, places, and concepts.

Online 99 Cents

http://www.JustTheFacts101.com

Use www.JustTheFacts101.com for all your study needs

including Facts101's online interactive problem solving labs in

chemistry, statistics, mathematics, and more.

CHAPTER OUTLINE: KEY TERMS, PEOPLE, PLACES, CONCEPTS

_____ | Expected value

_____ | Probability

_____ | Value

_____ | Pythagorean theorem

_____ | Statistic

_____ | Theorem

_____ | Constant

_____ | Standard deviation

_____ | Variance

_____ | Deviation

_____ | Independence

_____ | Mean

_____ | T-test

_____ | Complement

_____ | Binomial

_____ | Distribution

_____ | Condition

_____ | Regression

_____ | Probability density function

13. Random Variables and Probability Models

Expected value	In probability theory, the expected value refers, intuitively, to the value of a random variable one would 'expect' to find if one could repeat the random variable process an infinite number of times and take the average of the values obtained. More formally, the expected value is a weighted average of all possible values. In other words, each possible value that the random variable can assume is multiplied by its assigned weight, and the resulting products are then added together to find the expected value.
Probability	Probability is a measure of the likeliness that an event will occur. Probability is used to quantify an attitude of mind towards some proposition of whose truth we are not certain. The proposition of interest is usually of the form 'Will a specific event occur?' The attitude of mind is of the form 'How certain are we that the event will occur?' The certainty we adopt can be described in terms of a numerical measure and this number, between 0 and 1 (where 0 indicates impossibility and 1 indicates certainty), we call probability.
Value	In ethics, value denotes something's degree of importance, with the aim of determining what action or life is best to do or live, or at least attempt to describe the value of different actions (Axiology). It may be described as treating actions themselves as abstract objects, putting value to them. It deals with right conduct and good life, in the sense that a highly, or at least relatively highly, valuable action may be regarded as ethically 'good' (adjective sense), and an action of low, or at least relatively low, value may be regarded as 'bad'.
Pythagorean theorem	In mathematics, the Pythagorean theorem--or Pythagoras' theorem--is a relation in Euclidean geometry among the three sides of a right triangle. It states that the square of the hypotenuse (the side opposite the right angle) is equal to the sum of the squares of the other two sides. The theorem can be written as an equation relating the lengths of the sides a, b and c, often called the Pythagorean equation: $a^2 + b^2 = c^2$ where c represents the length of the hypotenuse, and a and b represent the lengths of the other two sides.
Statistic	A statistic is a single measure of some attribute of a sample (e.g., its arithmetic mean value). It is calculated by applying a function (statistical algorithm) to the values of the items of the sample, which are known together as a set of data. More formally, statistical theory defines a statistic as a function of a sample where the function itself is independent of the sample's distribution; that is, the function can be stated before realization of the data.
Theorem	In mathematics, a theorem is a statement that has been proven on the basis of previously established statements, such as other theorems--and generally accepted statements, such as axioms.

The proof of a mathematical theorem is a logical argument for the theorem statement given in accord with the rules of a deductive system. The proof of a theorem is often interpreted as justification of the truth of the theorem statement.

Constant

In mathematics, the adjective constant means non-varying. The noun constant may have two different meanings. It may refer to a fixed and well defined number or other mathematical object.

Standard deviation

In statistics and probability theory, the standard deviation shows how much variation or dispersion from the average exists. A low standard deviation indicates that the data points tend to be very close to the mean (also called expected value); a high standard deviation indicates that the data points are spread out over a large range of values.

The standard deviation of a random variable, statistical population, data set, or probability distribution is the square root of its variance.

Variance

In probability theory and statistics, variance measures how far a set of numbers is spread out. (A variance of zero indicates that all the values are identical). Variance is always non-negative: A small variance indicates that the data points tend to be very close to the mean (expected value) and hence to each other, while a high variance indicates that the data points are very spread out from the mean and from each other.

Deviation

In mathematics and statistics, deviation is a measure of difference between the observed value of a variable and some other value, often that variable's mean. The sign of the deviation reports the direction of that difference (the deviation is positive when the observed value exceeds the reference value). The magnitude of the value indicates the size of the difference.

Independence

In probability theory, to say that two events are independent means that the occurrence of one does not affect the probability of the other. Similarly, two random variables are independent if the realization of one does not affect the probability distribution of the other.

The concept of independence extends to dealing with collections of more than two events or random variables.

Mean

In probability and statistics, mean and expected value are used synonymously to refer to one measure of the central tendency either of a probability distribution or of the random variable characterized by that distribution. In the case of a discrete probability distribution of a random variable X, the mean is equal to the sum over every possible value weighted by the probability of that value; that is, it is computed by taking the product of each possible value x of X and its probability P(x), and then adding all these products together, giving

$$\mu = \sum x P(x)$$

13. Random Variables and Probability Models

T-test	A t-test is any statistical hypothesis test in which the test statistic follows a Student's t distribution if the null hypothesis is supported. It can be used to determine if two sets of data are significantly different from each other, and is most commonly applied when the test statistic would follow a normal distribution if the value of a scaling term in the test statistic were known. When the scaling term is unknown and is replaced by an estimate based on the data, the test statistic (under certain conditions) follows a Student's t distribution.
Complement	In set theory, a complement of a set A refers to things not in A. The relative complement of A with respect to a set B is the set of elements in B but not in A. When all sets under consideration are considered to be subsets of a given set U, the absolute complement of A is the set of all elements in U but not in A.
Binomial	In algebra, a binomial is a polynomial which is the sum of two terms, which are monomials. It is the simplest kind of polynomial after the monomials.
Distribution	In algebra and number theory, a distribution is a function on a system of finite sets into an abelian group which is analogous to an integral: it is thus the algebraic analogue of a distribution in the sense of generalised function. The original examples of distributions occur, unnamed, as functions f on Q/Z satisfying $$\sum_{r=0}^{N-1} \phi\left(x + \frac{r}{N}\right) = \phi(Nx) .$$ We shall call these ordinary distributions. They also occur in p-adic integration theory in Iwasawa theory.
Condition	Comprehensive treatment of the word 'condition' requires emphasizing that it is ambiguous in the sense of having multiple normal meanings and that its meanings are often vague in the sense of admitting borderline cases. According to the 2007 American Philosophy: an Encyclopedia, in one widely used sense, conditions are or resemble qualities, properties, features, characteristics, or attributes. In these senses, a condition is often denoted by a nominalization of a grammatical predicate: 'being equilateral' is a nominalization of the predicate 'is equilateral'.
Regression	Regression in medicine is a characteristic of diseases to show lighter symptoms without completely disappearing. At a later point, symptoms may return. These symptoms are then called recidive.
Probability density function	In probability theory, a probability density function, or density of a continuous random variable, is a function that describes the relative likelihood for this random variable to take on a given value.

The probability of the random variable falling within a particular range of values is given by the integral of this variable's density over that range--that is, it is given by the area under the density function but above the horizontal axis and between the lowest and greatest values of the range. The probability density function is nonnegative everywhere, and its integral over the entire space is equal to one.

CHAPTER QUIZ: KEY TERMS, PEOPLE, PLACES, CONCEPTS

1. A _____ is a single measure of some attribute of a sample (e.g., its arithmetic mean value). It is calculated by applying a function (statistical algorithm) to the values of the items of the sample, which are known together as a set of data.

   More formally, statistical theory defines a _____ as a function of a sample where the function itself is independent of the sample's distribution; that is, the function can be stated before realization of the data.

   a. Statistic
   b. L-statistic
   c. Parameter space
   d. Pivotal quantity

2. _____ is a measure of the likeliness that an event will occur.

   _____ is used to quantify an attitude of mind towards some proposition of whose truth we are not certain. The proposition of interest is usually of the form 'Will a specific event occur?' The attitude of mind is of the form 'How certain are we that the event will occur?' The certainty we adopt can be described in terms of a numerical measure and this number, between 0 and 1 (where 0 indicates impossibility and 1 indicates certainty), we call _____.

   a. Probability
   b. Marginal structural model
   c. Research
   d. Design science

3. . In probability theory, a _____, or density of a continuous random variable, is a function that describes the relative likelihood for this random variable to take on a given value. The probability of the random variable falling within a particular range of values is given by the integral of this variable's density over that range--that is, it is given by the area under the density function but above the horizontal axis and between the lowest and greatest values of the range. The _____ is nonnegative everywhere, and its integral over the entire space is equal to one.

   a. Central moment
   b. Characteristic function

c. Probability density function

d. Combinant

4. In probability theory, the _____ refers, intuitively, to the value of a random variable one would 'expect' to find if one could repeat the random variable process an infinite number of times and take the average of the values obtained. More formally, the _____ is a weighted average of all possible values. In other words, each possible value that the random variable can assume is multiplied by its assigned weight, and the resulting products are then added together to find the _____.

a. Expected value

b. Characteristic function

c. Coefficient of variation

d. Combinant

5. Comprehensive treatment of the word '_____' requires emphasizing that it is ambiguous in the sense of having multiple normal meanings and that its meanings are often vague in the sense of admitting borderline cases.

According to the 2007 American Philosophy: an Encyclopedia, in one widely used sense, _____s are or resemble qualities, properties, features, characteristics, or attributes. In these senses, a _____ is often denoted by a nominalization of a grammatical predicate: 'being equilateral' is a nominalization of the predicate 'is equilateral'.

a. Belief revision

b. Boolean network

c. Condition

d. Ceqli

1. a

2. a

3. c

4. a

5. c

You can take the complete Chapter Practice Test

for 13. Random Variables and Probability Models
on all key terms, persons, places, and concepts.

Online 99 Cents

http://www.JustTheFacts101.com

Use www.JustTheFacts101.com for all your study needs

including Facts101's online interactive problem solving labs in

chemistry, statistics, mathematics, and more.

14. Sampling Distribution Models

CHAPTER OUTLINE: KEY TERMS, PEOPLE, PLACES, CONCEPTS

_____ Central limit theorem

_____ Condition

_____ Sampling distribution

_____ Sample

_____ Sampling error

_____ Sampling

_____ Sample size

_____ Margin of error

_____ Distribution

_____ Regression

_____ Lottery

_____ Mean

_____ Law of large numbers

_____ Randomization

_____ Deviation

_____ Standard deviation

_____ Independence

14. Sampling Distribution Models

Central limit theorem	In probability theory, the central limit theorem states that, given certain conditions, the arithmetic mean of a sufficiently large number of iterates of independent random variables, each with a well-defined expected value and well-defined variance, will be approximately normally distributed. That is, suppose that a sample is obtained containing a large number of observations, each observation being randomly generated in a way that does not depend on the values of the other observations, and that the arithmetic average of the observed values is computed. If this procedure is performed many times, the central limit theorem says that the computed values of the average will be distributed according to the normal distribution (commonly known as a 'bell curve').
Condition	Comprehensive treatment of the word 'condition' requires emphasizing that it is ambiguous in the sense of having multiple normal meanings and that its meanings are often vague in the sense of admitting borderline cases. According to the 2007 American Philosophy: an Encyclopedia, in one widely used sense, conditions are or resemble qualities, properties, features, characteristics, or attributes. In these senses, a condition is often denoted by a nominalization of a grammatical predicate: 'being equilateral' is a nominalization of the predicate 'is equilateral'.
Sampling distribution	In statistics, a sampling distribution or finite-sample distribution is the probability distribution of a given statistic based on a random sample. Sampling distributions are important in statistics because they provide a major simplification on the route to statistical inference. More specifically, they allow analytical considerations to be based on the sampling distribution of a statistic, rather than on the joint probability distribution of all the individual sample values.
Sample	In statistics and quantitative research methodology, a data sample is a set of data collected and/or selected from a statistical population by a defined procedure.
Sampling error	In statistics, sampling error is incurred when the statistical characteristics of a population are estimated from a subset, or sample, of that population. Since the sample does not include all members of the population, statistics on the sample, such as means and quantiles, generally differ from parameters on the entire population. For example, if one measures the height of a thousand individuals from a country of one million, the average height of the thousand is typically not the same as the average height of all one million people in the country.
Sampling	In statistics, quality assurance, & survey methodology, sampling is concerned with the selection of a subset of individuals from within a statistical population to estimate characteristics of the whole population. Each observation measures one or more properties (such as weight, location, color) of observable bodies distinguished as independent objects or individuals. In survey sampling, weights can be applied to the data to adjust for the sample design, particularly stratified sampling.
Sample size	Sample size determination is the act of choosing the number of observations or replicates to include in a statistical sample.

14. Sampling Distribution Models

The sample size is an important feature of any empirical study in which the goal is to make inferences about a population from a sample. In practice, the sample size used in a study is determined based on the expense of data collection, and the need to have sufficient statistical power.

Margin of error	The margin of error is a statistic expressing the amount of random sampling error in a survey's results. The larger the margin of error, the less confidence one should have that the poll's reported results are close to the 'true' figures; that is, the figures for the whole population. Margin of error occurs whenever a population is incompletely sampled.

Distribution

In algebra and number theory, a distribution is a function on a system of finite sets into an abelian group which is analogous to an integral: it is thus the algebraic analogue of a distribution in the sense of generalised function.

The original examples of distributions occur, unnamed, as functions f on Q/Z satisfying

$$\sum_{r=0}^{N-1} \phi\left(x + \frac{r}{N}\right) = \phi(Nx) \ .$$

We shall call these ordinary distributions. They also occur in p-adic integration theory in Iwasawa theory.

Regression

Regression in medicine is a characteristic of diseases to show lighter symptoms without completely disappearing. At a later point, symptoms may return. These symptoms are then called recidive.

Lottery

In expected utility theory, a lottery is a discrete distribution of probability on a set of states of nature. The elements of a lottery correspond to the probability that a certain outcome arises from a given state of nature. In economics, individuals are assumed to rank lotteries according to a rational system of preferences, although it is now accepted that people make irrational choices systematically.

Mean

In probability and statistics, mean and expected value are used synonymously to refer to one measure of the central tendency either of a probability distribution or of the random variable characterized by that distribution. In the case of a discrete probability distribution of a random variable X, the mean is equal to the sum over every possible value weighted by the probability of that value; that is, it is computed by taking the product of each possible value x of X and its probability P(x), and then adding all these products together, giving

$$\mu = \sum xP(x)$$

Law of large numbers

In probability theory, the law of large numbers is a theorem that describes the result of performing the same experiment a large number of times.

14. Sampling Distribution Models

According to the law, the average of the results obtained from a large number of trials should be close to the expected value, and will tend to become closer as more trials are performed.

The LLN is important because it 'guarantees' stable long-term results for the averages of random events.

Randomization

Randomization is the process of making something random; this means:

Randomization is not haphazard. Instead, a random process is a sequence of random variables describing a process whose outcomes do not follow a deterministic pattern, but follow an evolution described by probability distributions. For example, a random sample of individuals from a population refers to a sample where every individual has a known probability of being sampled.

Deviation

In mathematics and statistics, deviation is a measure of difference between the observed value of a variable and some other value, often that variable's mean. The sign of the deviation reports the direction of that difference (the deviation is positive when the observed value exceeds the reference value). The magnitude of the value indicates the size of the difference.

Standard deviation

In statistics and probability theory, the standard deviation shows how much variation or dispersion from the average exists. A low standard deviation indicates that the data points tend to be very close to the mean (also called expected value); a high standard deviation indicates that the data points are spread out over a large range of values.

The standard deviation of a random variable, statistical population, data set, or probability distribution is the square root of its variance.

Independence

In probability theory, to say that two events are independent means that the occurrence of one does not affect the probability of the other. Similarly, two random variables are independent if the realization of one does not affect the probability distribution of the other.

The concept of independence extends to dealing with collections of more than two events or random variables.

1. In statistics, _____ is incurred when the statistical characteristics of a population are estimated from a subset, or sample, of that population. Since the sample does not include all members of the population, statistics on the sample, such as means and quantiles, generally differ from parameters on the entire population. For example, if one measures the height of a thousand individuals from a country of one million, the average height of the thousand is typically not the same as the average height of all one million people in the country.

   a. Correct sampling
   b. Deep sampling
   c. Judgment sample
   d. Sampling error

2. In probability theory, the _____ states that, given certain conditions, the arithmetic mean of a sufficiently large number of iterates of independent random variables, each with a well-defined expected value and well-defined variance, will be approximately normally distributed. That is, suppose that a sample is obtained containing a large number of observations, each observation being randomly generated in a way that does not depend on the values of the other observations, and that the arithmetic average of the observed values is computed. If this procedure is performed many times, the _____ says that the computed values of the average will be distributed according to the normal distribution (commonly known as a 'bell curve').

   a. Covariance
   b. Law of total covariance
   c. Central limit theorem
   d. Law of total expectation

3. The _____ is a statistic expressing the amount of random sampling error in a survey's results. The larger the _____, the less confidence one should have that the poll's reported results are close to the 'true' figures; that is, the figures for the whole population. _____ occurs whenever a population is incompletely sampled.

   a. Berkson error model
   b. Margin of error
   c. Cosmic variance
   d. Fano factor

4. . Comprehensive treatment of the word '_____' requires emphasizing that it is ambiguous in the sense of having multiple normal meanings and that its meanings are often vague in the sense of admitting borderline cases.

   According to the 2007 American Philosophy: an Encyclopedia, in one widely used sense, _____s are or resemble qualities, properties, features, characteristics, or attributes. In these senses, a _____ is often denoted by a nominalization of a grammatical predicate: 'being equilateral' is a nominalization of the predicate 'is equilateral'.

   a. Belief revision
   b. Condition
   c. Canon

14. Sampling Distribution Models

5. In mathematics and statistics, _____ is a measure of difference between the observed value of a variable and some other value, often that variable's mean. The sign of the _____ reports the direction of that difference (the _____ is positive when the observed value exceeds the reference value). The magnitude of the value indicates the size of the difference.

    a. Ceiling effect
    b. Deviation
    c. Consistency
    d. Cost-of-living index

1. d
2. c
3. b
4. b
5. b

You can take the complete Chapter Practice Test

for 14. Sampling Distribution Models
on all key terms, persons, places, and concepts.

Online 99 Cents

http://www.JustTheFacts101.com

Use www.JustTheFacts101.com for all your study needs

including Facts101's online interactive problem solving labs in

chemistry, statistics, mathematics, and more.

CHAPTER OUTLINE: KEY TERMS, PEOPLE, PLACES, CONCEPTS

Condition

Standard error

Error

Sampling

Sampling distribution

Difference

Margin of error

Theorem

Randomization

Sample size

Distribution

Regression

Pilot study

15. Confidence Intervals for Proportions

Condition	Comprehensive treatment of the word 'condition' requires emphasizing that it is ambiguous in the sense of having multiple normal meanings and that its meanings are often vague in the sense of admitting borderline cases. According to the 2007 American Philosophy: an Encyclopedia, in one widely used sense, conditions are or resemble qualities, properties, features, characteristics, or attributes. In these senses, a condition is often denoted by a nominalization of a grammatical predicate: 'being equilateral' is a nominalization of the predicate 'is equilateral'.
Standard error	The standard error is the standard deviation of the sampling distribution of a statistic. The term may also be used to refer to an estimate of that standard deviation, derived from a particular sample used to compute the estimate. For example, the sample mean is the usual estimator of a population mean.
Error	The word error entails different meanings and usages relative to how it is conceptually applied. The concrete meaning of the Latin word 'error' is 'wandering' or 'straying'. Unlike an illusion, an error or a mistake can sometimes be dispelled through knowledge (knowing that one is looking at a mirage and not at real water does not make the mirage disappear).
Sampling	In statistics, quality assurance, & survey methodology, sampling is concerned with the selection of a subset of individuals from within a statistical population to estimate characteristics of the whole population. Each observation measures one or more properties (such as weight, location, color) of observable bodies distinguished as independent objects or individuals. In survey sampling, weights can be applied to the data to adjust for the sample design, particularly stratified sampling.
Sampling distribution	In statistics, a sampling distribution or finite-sample distribution is the probability distribution of a given statistic based on a random sample. Sampling distributions are important in statistics because they provide a major simplification on the route to statistical inference. More specifically, they allow analytical considerations to be based on the sampling distribution of a statistic, rather than on the joint probability distribution of all the individual sample values.
Difference	Difference is a key concept of philosophy, denoting the process or set of properties by which one entity is distinguished from another within a relational field or a given conceptual system. In the Western philosophical system, difference is traditionally viewed as being opposed to identity, following the Principles of Leibniz, and in particular his Law of the Identity of indiscernibles. In structuralist and poststructuralist accounts, however, difference is understood to be constitutive of both meaning and identity.
Margin of error	The margin of error is a statistic expressing the amount of random sampling error in a survey's results. The larger the margin of error, the less confidence one should have that the poll's reported results are close to the 'true' figures; that is, the figures for the whole population.

| Theorem | In mathematics, a theorem is a statement that has been proven on the basis of previously established statements, such as other theorems--and generally accepted statements, such as axioms. The proof of a mathematical theorem is a logical argument for the theorem statement given in accord with the rules of a deductive system. The proof of a theorem is often interpreted as justification of the truth of the theorem statement. |

| Randomization | Randomization is the process of making something random; this means:

Randomization is not haphazard. Instead, a random process is a sequence of random variables describing a process whose outcomes do not follow a deterministic pattern, but follow an evolution described by probability distributions. For example, a random sample of individuals from a population refers to a sample where every individual has a known probability of being sampled. |

| Sample size | Sample size determination is the act of choosing the number of observations or replicates to include in a statistical sample. The sample size is an important feature of any empirical study in which the goal is to make inferences about a population from a sample. In practice, the sample size used in a study is determined based on the expense of data collection, and the need to have sufficient statistical power. |

| Distribution | In algebra and number theory, a distribution is a function on a system of finite sets into an abelian group which is analogous to an integral: it is thus the algebraic analogue of a distribution in the sense of generalised function.

The original examples of distributions occur, unnamed, as functions f on Q/Z

$$\text{satisfying} \sum_{r=0}^{N-1} \phi \left(x + \frac{r}{N} \right) = \phi(Nx) \ .$$

We shall call these ordinary distributions. They also occur in p-adic integration theory in Iwasawa theory. |

| Regression | Regression in medicine is a characteristic of diseases to show lighter symptoms without completely disappearing. At a later point, symptoms may return. These symptoms are then called recidive. |

| Pilot study | A pilot experiment, also called a pilot study, is a small scale preliminary study conducted in order to evaluate feasibility, time, cost, adverse events, and effect size in an attempt to predict an appropriate sample size and improve upon the study design prior to performance of a full-scale research project. Pilot studies, therefore, may not be appropriate for case studies. |

15. Confidence Intervals for Proportions

1. A pilot experiment, also called a _____, is a small scale preliminary study conducted in order to evaluate feasibility, time, cost, adverse events, and effect size in an attempt to predict an appropriate sample size and improve upon the study design prior to performance of a full-scale research project. _____(ies), therefore, may not be appropriate for case studies.

    a. Blind taste test
    b. Construct
    c. Discovery science
    d. Pilot study

2. _____ is the process of making something random; this means:

    _____ is not haphazard. Instead, a random process is a sequence of random variables describing a process whose outcomes do not follow a deterministic pattern, but follow an evolution described by probability distributions. For example, a random sample of individuals from a population refers to a sample where every individual has a known probability of being sampled.

    a. Determinism
    b. Global Consciousness Project
    c. Randomization
    d. Nothing up my sleeve number

3. The word _____ entails different meanings and usages relative to how it is conceptually applied. The concrete meaning of the Latin word '_____' is 'wandering' or 'straying'. Unlike an illusion, an _____ or a mistake can sometimes be dispelled through knowledge (knowing that one is looking at a mirage and not at real water does not make the mirage disappear).

    a. Error
    b. Baculometry
    c. Basal area
    d. Berkson error model

4. In statistics, quality assurance, & survey methodology, _____ is concerned with the selection of a subset of individuals from within a statistical population to estimate characteristics of the whole population. Each observation measures one or more properties (such as weight, location, color) of observable bodies distinguished as independent objects or individuals. In survey _____, weights can be applied to the data to adjust for the sample design, particularly stratified _____.

    a. Covariance
    b. Law of total covariance
    c. Sampling
    d. Law of total expectation

5. . In algebra and number theory, a _____ is a function on a system of finite sets into an abelian group which is analogous to an integral: it is thus the algebraic analogue of a _____ in the sense of generalised function.

The original examples of _____s occur, unnamed, as functions f on Q/Z

satisfying $$\sum_{r=0}^{N-1} \phi\left(x + \frac{r}{N}\right) = \phi(Nx) \ .$$

We shall call these ordinary _____s. They also occur in p-adic integration theory in Iwasawa theory.

a. Binomial
b. Canonical form
c. Distribution
d. Cluster algebra

1. d
2. c
3. a
4. c
5. c

You can take the complete Chapter Practice Test

for 15. Confidence Intervals for Proportions
on all key terms, persons, places, and concepts.

Online 99 Cents

http://www.JustTheFacts101.com

Use www.JustTheFacts101.com for all your study needs

including Facts101's online interactive problem solving labs in

chemistry, statistics, mathematics, and more.

16. Testing Hypotheses About Proportions

_____ | P-value

_____ | Theorem

_____ | Difference

_____ | Error

_____ | Power

_____ | Standard error

_____ | Alternative hypothesis

_____ | Null hypothesis

_____ | Regression

_____ | Conditional probability

_____ | Null

_____ | Probability

_____ | Blocking

_____ | Value

_____ | Hypothesis

_____ | Sampling

_____ | Condition

_____ | Mean

P-value	In statistical significance testing, the p-value is the probability of obtaining a test statistic at least as extreme as the one that was actually observed, assuming that the null hypothesis is true. A researcher will often 'reject the null hypothesis' when the p-value turns out to be less than a certain significance level, often 0.05 or 0.01. Such a result indicates that the observed result would be highly unlikely under the null hypothesis. Many common statistical tests, such as chi-squared tests or Student's t-test, produce test statistics which can be interpreted using p-values.
Theorem	In mathematics, a theorem is a statement that has been proven on the basis of previously established statements, such as other theorems--and generally accepted statements, such as axioms. The proof of a mathematical theorem is a logical argument for the theorem statement given in accord with the rules of a deductive system. The proof of a theorem is often interpreted as justification of the truth of the theorem statement.
Difference	Difference is a key concept of philosophy, denoting the process or set of properties by which one entity is distinguished from another within a relational field or a given conceptual system. In the Western philosophical system, difference is traditionally viewed as being opposed to identity, following the Principles of Leibniz, and in particular his Law of the Identity of indiscernibles. In structuralist and poststructuralist accounts, however, difference is understood to be constitutive of both meaning and identity.
Error	The word error entails different meanings and usages relative to how it is conceptually applied. The concrete meaning of the Latin word 'error' is 'wandering' or 'straying'. Unlike an illusion, an error or a mistake can sometimes be dispelled through knowledge (knowing that one is looking at a mirage and not at real water does not make the mirage disappear).
Power	In physics, power is the rate of doing work. It is equivalent to an amount of energy consumed per unit time. In the MKS system, the unit of power is the joule per second (J/s), known as the watt in honor of James Watt, the eighteenth-century developer of the steam engine.
Standard error	The standard error is the standard deviation of the sampling distribution of a statistic. The term may also be used to refer to an estimate of that standard deviation, derived from a particular sample used to compute the estimate. For example, the sample mean is the usual estimator of a population mean.
Alternative hypothesis	In statistical hypothesis testing, the alternative hypothesis and the null hypothesis are the two rival hypotheses which are compared by a statistical hypothesis test. An example might be where water quality in a stream has been observed over many years and a test is made of the null hypothesis that there is no change in quality between the first and second halves of the data against the alternative hypothesis that the quality is poorer in the second half of the record. In the case of a scalar parameter, there are four principal types of alternative hypothesis:•Point.

16. Testing Hypotheses About Proportions

Point alternative hypotheses occur when the hypothesis test is framed so that the population distribution under the alternative hypothesis is a fully defined distribution, with no unknown parameters; such hypotheses are usually of no practical interest but are fundamental to theoretical considerations of statistical inference and are the basis of the Neyman-Pearson lemma.•One-tailed directional. A one-tailed directional alternative hypothesis is concerned with the region of rejection for only one tail of the sampling distribution.•Two-tailed directional. A two-tailed directional alternative hypothesis is concerned with both regions of rejection of the sampling distribution.•Non-directional. A non-directional alternative hypothesis is not concerned with either region of rejection, but, rather, it is only concerned that null hypothesis is not true.

Null hypothesis	In statistical inference of observed data of a scientific experiment, the null hypothesis refers to a general or default position: that there is no relationship between two measured phenomena, or that a potential medical treatment has no effect. Rejecting or disproving the null hypothesis - and thus concluding that there are grounds for believing that there is a relationship between two phenomena or that a potential treatment has a measurable effect - is a central task in the modern practice of science, and gives a precise sense in which a claim is capable of being proven false. In statistical significance, the null hypothesis is often denoted H_0 (read "H-nought" in Britain or 'H-zero' in America), and is generally assumed true until evidence indicates otherwise (e.g., H_0: μ = 500 hours).
Regression	Regression in medicine is a characteristic of diseases to show lighter symptoms without completely disappearing. At a later point, symptoms may return. These symptoms are then called recidive.
Conditional probability	In probability theory, a conditional probability measures the probability of an event given that another event has occurred. If the events are A and B respectively, this is said to be 'the probability of A given B'. It is commonly denoted by P(A\B), or sometimes $P_B(A)$.
Null	In mathematics, the word null means of or related to having zero members in a set or a value of zero. Sometimes the symbol Ø is used to distinguish 'null' from 0. In a normed vector space the null vector is the zero vector; in a seminormed vector space such as Minkowski space, null vectors are, in general, non-zero.
Probability	Probability is a measure of the likeliness that an event will occur. Probability is used to quantify an attitude of mind towards some proposition of whose truth we are not certain. The proposition of interest is usually of the form 'Will a specific event occur?' The attitude of mind is of the form 'How certain are we that the event will occur?' The certainty we adopt can be described in terms of a numerical measure and this number, between 0 and 1 (where 0 indicates impossibility and 1 indicates certainty), we call probability.

16. Testing Hypotheses About Proportions

CHAPTER HIGHLIGHTS & NOTES: KEY TERMS, PEOPLE, PLACES, CONCEPTS

Blocking	In the statistical theory of the design of experiments, blocking is the arranging of experimental units in groups that are similar to one another. For example, an experiment is designed to test a new drug on patients. There are two levels of the treatment, drug, and placebo, administered to male and female patients in a double blind trial.
Value	In ethics, value denotes something's degree of importance, with the aim of determining what action or life is best to do or live, or at least attempt to describe the value of different actions (Axiology). It may be described as treating actions themselves as abstract objects, putting value to them. It deals with right conduct and good life, in the sense that a highly, or at least relatively highly, valuable action may be regarded as ethically 'good' (adjective sense), and an action of low, or at least relatively low, value may be regarded as 'bad'.
Hypothesis	A hypothesis is a proposed explanation for a phenomenon. For a hypothesis to be a scientific hypothesis, the scientific method requires that one can test it. Scientists generally base scientific hypotheses on previous observations that cannot satisfactorily be explained with the available scientific theories.
Sampling	In statistics, quality assurance, & survey methodology, sampling is concerned with the selection of a subset of individuals from within a statistical population to estimate characteristics of the whole population. Each observation measures one or more properties (such as weight, location, color) of observable bodies distinguished as independent objects or individuals. In survey sampling, weights can be applied to the data to adjust for the sample design, particularly stratified sampling.
Condition	Comprehensive treatment of the word 'condition' requires emphasizing that it is ambiguous in the sense of having multiple normal meanings and that its meanings are often vague in the sense of admitting borderline cases. According to the 2007 American Philosophy: an Encyclopedia, in one widely used sense, conditions are or resemble qualities, properties, features, characteristics, or attributes. In these senses, a condition is often denoted by a nominalization of a grammatical predicate: 'being equilateral' is a nominalization of the predicate 'is equilateral'.
Mean	In probability and statistics, mean and expected value are used synonymously to refer to one measure of the central tendency either of a probability distribution or of the random variable characterized by that distribution. In the case of a discrete probability distribution of a random variable X, the mean is equal to the sum over every possible value weighted by the probability of that value; that is, it is computed by taking the product of each possible value x of X and its probability $P(x)$, and then adding all these products together, giving $$\mu = \sum x P(x)$$

16. Testing Hypotheses About Proportions

1. _____ is a key concept of philosophy, denoting the process or set of properties by which one entity is distinguished from another within a relational field or a given conceptual system. In the Western philosophical system, _____ is traditionally viewed as being opposed to identity, following the Principles of Leibniz, and in particular his Law of the Identity of indiscernibles. In structuralist and poststructuralist accounts, however, _____ is understood to be constitutive of both meaning and identity.

   a. Belief revision
   b. Difference
   c. Canon
   d. Ceqli

2. Comprehensive treatment of the word '_____' requires emphasizing that it is ambiguous in the sense of having multiple normal meanings and that its meanings are often vague in the sense of admitting borderline cases.

   According to the 2007 American Philosophy: an Encyclopedia, in one widely used sense, _____s are or resemble qualities, properties, features, characteristics, or attributes. In these senses, a _____ is often denoted by a nominalization of a grammatical predicate: 'being equilateral' is a nominalization of the predicate 'is equilateral'.

   a. Belief revision
   b. Boolean network
   c. Canon
   d. Condition

3. _____ in medicine is a characteristic of diseases to show lighter symptoms without completely disappearing. At a later point, symptoms may return. These symptoms are then called recidive.

   a. 1947 New York City smallpox outbreak
   b. 1993 Four Corners hantavirus outbreak
   c. 2003 Midwest monkeypox outbreak
   d. Regression

4. In ethics, _____ denotes something's degree of importance, with the aim of determining what action or life is best to do or live, or at least attempt to describe the _____ of different actions (Axiology). It may be described as treating actions themselves as abstract objects, putting _____ to them. It deals with right conduct and good life, in the sense that a highly, or at least relatively highly, valuable action may be regarded as ethically 'good' (adjective sense), and an action of low, or at least relatively low, _____ may be regarded as 'bad'.

   a. Bad faith
   b. Value
   c. Common good
   d. Conscience

5. . In physics, _____ is the rate of doing work. It is equivalent to an amount of energy consumed per unit time.

In the MKS system, the unit of _____ is the joule per second (J/s), known as the watt in honor of James Watt, the eighteenth-century developer of the steam engine.

a. Bloch wave
b. Power
c. Bohr model
d. Boiling point

1. b
2. d
3. d
4. b
5. b

CHAPTER OUTLINE: KEY TERMS, PEOPLE, PLACES, CONCEPTS

	Inference
	Central limit theorem
	Sample
	Sample size
	Difference
	Error
	Margin of error
	Sampling distribution
	Standard error
	Condition
	Confidence interval
	Degrees of freedom
	Theorem
	Mean
	Sampling
	T-test
	Student's t
	Distribution
	Census
	Complement
	Conditional probability

17. Inferences About Means

Probability

P-value

Hypothesis

Power

Pilot study

Size

Multimodal distribution

Randomization

Statistical significance

CHAPTER HIGHLIGHTS & NOTES: KEY TERMS, PEOPLE, PLACES, CONCEPTS

Inference	Inference is the act or process of deriving logical conclusions from premises known or assumed to be true. The conclusion drawn is also called an idiomatic. The laws of valid inference are studied in the field of logic.
Central limit theorem	In probability theory, the central limit theorem states that, given certain conditions, the arithmetic mean of a sufficiently large number of iterates of independent random variables, each with a well-defined expected value and well-defined variance, will be approximately normally distributed. That is, suppose that a sample is obtained containing a large number of observations, each observation being randomly generated in a way that does not depend on the values of the other observations, and that the arithmetic average of the observed values is computed. If this procedure is performed many times, the central limit theorem says that the computed values of the average will be distributed according to the normal distribution (commonly known as a 'bell curve').
Sample	In statistics and quantitative research methodology, a data sample is a set of data collected and/or selected from a statistical population by a defined procedure.

17. Inferences About Means

Sample size	Sample size determination is the act of choosing the number of observations or replicates to include in a statistical sample. The sample size is an important feature of any empirical study in which the goal is to make inferences about a population from a sample. In practice, the sample size used in a study is determined based on the expense of data collection, and the need to have sufficient statistical power.
Difference	Difference is a key concept of philosophy, denoting the process or set of properties by which one entity is distinguished from another within a relational field or a given conceptual system. In the Western philosophical system, difference is traditionally viewed as being opposed to identity, following the Principles of Leibniz, and in particular his Law of the Identity of indiscernibles. In structuralist and poststructuralist accounts, however, difference is understood to be constitutive of both meaning and identity.
Error	The word error entails different meanings and usages relative to how it is conceptually applied. The concrete meaning of the Latin word 'error' is 'wandering' or 'straying'. Unlike an illusion, an error or a mistake can sometimes be dispelled through knowledge (knowing that one is looking at a mirage and not at real water does not make the mirage disappear).
Margin of error	The margin of error is a statistic expressing the amount of random sampling error in a survey's results. The larger the margin of error, the less confidence one should have that the poll's reported results are close to the 'true' figures; that is, the figures for the whole population. Margin of error occurs whenever a population is incompletely sampled.
Sampling distribution	In statistics, a sampling distribution or finite-sample distribution is the probability distribution of a given statistic based on a random sample. Sampling distributions are important in statistics because they provide a major simplification on the route to statistical inference. More specifically, they allow analytical considerations to be based on the sampling distribution of a statistic, rather than on the joint probability distribution of all the individual sample values.
Standard error	The standard error is the standard deviation of the sampling distribution of a statistic. The term may also be used to refer to an estimate of that standard deviation, derived from a particular sample used to compute the estimate.

For example, the sample mean is the usual estimator of a population mean. |
| Condition | Comprehensive treatment of the word 'condition' requires emphasizing that it is ambiguous in the sense of having multiple normal meanings and that its meanings are often vague in the sense of admitting borderline cases.

According to the 2007 American Philosophy: an Encyclopedia, in one widely used sense, conditions are or resemble qualities, properties, features, characteristics, or attributes. |

17. Inferences About Means

Confidence interval	In statistical inference, the concept of a confidence distribution has often been loosely referred to as a distribution function on the parameter space that can represent confidence intervals of all levels for a parameter of interest. Historically, it has typically been constructed by inverting the upper limits of lower sided confidence intervals of all levels, and it was also commonly associated with a fiducial interpretation (fiducial distribution), although it is a purely frequentist concept. A confidence distribution is not a valid probability distribution, but may still be a function useful for making inferences.
Degrees of freedom	In many scientific fields, the degrees of freedom of a system is the number of parameters of the system that may vary independently. For example, the position of a figure in the plane has three degrees of freedom: its orientation and the two coordinates of any fixed point of the figure. In mathematics, this notion is formalized as the dimension of a manifold or an algebraic variety.
Theorem	In mathematics, a theorem is a statement that has been proven on the basis of previously established statements, such as other theorems--and generally accepted statements, such as axioms. The proof of a mathematical theorem is a logical argument for the theorem statement given in accord with the rules of a deductive system. The proof of a theorem is often interpreted as justification of the truth of the theorem statement.
Mean	In probability and statistics, mean and expected value are used synonymously to refer to one measure of the central tendency either of a probability distribution or of the random variable characterized by that distribution. In the case of a discrete probability distribution of a random variable X, the mean is equal to the sum over every possible value weighted by the probability of that value; that is, it is computed by taking the product of each possible value x of X and its probability P(x), and then adding all these products together, giving $$\mu = \sum x P(x)$$
Sampling	In statistics, quality assurance, & survey methodology, sampling is concerned with the selection of a subset of individuals from within a statistical population to estimate characteristics of the whole population. Each observation measures one or more properties (such as weight, location, color) of observable bodies distinguished as independent objects or individuals. In survey sampling, weights can be applied to the data to adjust for the sample design, particularly stratified sampling.
T-test	A t-test is any statistical hypothesis test in which the test statistic follows a Student's t distribution if the null hypothesis is supported. It can be used to determine if two sets of data are significantly different from each other, and is most commonly applied when the test statistic would follow a normal distribution if the value of a scaling term in the test statistic were known. When the scaling term is unknown and is replaced by an estimate based on the data, the test statistic (under certain conditions) follows a Student's t distribution.

17. Inferences About Means

Student's t

In probability and statistics, Student's t-distribution is a family of continuous probability distributions that arise when estimating the mean of a normally distributed population in situations where the sample size is small and population standard deviation is unknown. It plays a role in a number of widely used statistical analyses, including the Student's t-test for assessing the statistical significance of the difference between two sample means, the construction of confidence intervals for the difference between two population means, and in linear regression analysis. The Student's t-distribution also arises in the Bayesian analysis of data from a normal family.

Distribution

In algebra and number theory, a distribution is a function on a system of finite sets into an abelian group which is analogous to an integral: it is thus the algebraic analogue of a distribution in the sense of generalised function.

The original examples of distributions occur, unnamed, as functions f on Q/Z

$$\sum_{r=0}^{N-1} \phi\left(x + \frac{r}{N}\right) = \phi(Nx) \ .$$

satisfying

We shall call these ordinary distributions. They also occur in p-adic integration theory in Iwasawa theory.

Census

A census is the procedure of systematically acquiring and recording information about the members of a given population. It is a regularly occurring and official count of a particular population. The term is used mostly in connection with national population and housing censuses; other common censuses include agriculture, business, and traffic censuses.

Complement

In set theory, a complement of a set A refers to things not in A. The relative complement of A with respect to a set B is the set of elements in B but not in A. When all sets under consideration are considered to be subsets of a given set U, the absolute complement of A is the set of all elements in U but not in A.

Conditional probability

In probability theory, a conditional probability measures the probability of an event given that another event has occurred. If the events are A and B respectively, this is said to be 'the probability of A given B'. It is commonly denoted by $P(A \backslash B)$, or sometimes $P_B(A)$.

Probability

Probability is a measure of the likeliness that an event will occur.

Probability is used to quantify an attitude of mind towards some proposition of whose truth we are not certain. The proposition of interest is usually of the form 'Will a specific event occur?' The attitude of mind is of the form 'How certain are we that the event will occur?' The certainty we adopt can be described in terms of a numerical measure and this number, between 0 and 1 (where 0 indicates impossibility and 1 indicates certainty), we call probability.

17. Inferences About Means

P-value	In statistical significance testing, the p-value is the probability of obtaining a test statistic at least as extreme as the one that was actually observed, assuming that the null hypothesis is true. A researcher will often 'reject the null hypothesis' when the p-value turns out to be less than a certain significance level, often 0.05 or 0.01. Such a result indicates that the observed result would be highly unlikely under the null hypothesis. Many common statistical tests, such as chi-squared tests or Student's t-test, produce test statistics which can be interpreted using p-values.
Hypothesis	A hypothesis is a proposed explanation for a phenomenon. For a hypothesis to be a scientific hypothesis, the scientific method requires that one can test it. Scientists generally base scientific hypotheses on previous observations that cannot satisfactorily be explained with the available scientific theories.
Power	In physics, power is the rate of doing work. It is equivalent to an amount of energy consumed per unit time. In the MKS system, the unit of power is the joule per second (J/s), known as the watt in honor of James Watt, the eighteenth-century developer of the steam engine.
Pilot study	A pilot experiment, also called a pilot study, is a small scale preliminary study conducted in order to evaluate feasibility, time, cost, adverse events, and effect size in an attempt to predict an appropriate sample size and improve upon the study design prior to performance of a full-scale research project. Pilot studies, therefore, may not be appropriate for case studies.
Size	In statistics, the size of a statistical test is the maximum of the probabilities of a type I error, i.e. of the probabilities of falsely rejecting the null hypothesis. In the case of a simple null hypothesis the size is the only possible probability of a type I error. The size of a test is denoted by the Greek letter a (alpha).
Multimodal distribution	In statistics, a multimodal distribution is a continuous probability distribution with two or more modes.
Randomization	Randomization is the process of making something random; this means:

Randomization is not haphazard. Instead, a random process is a sequence of random variables describing a process whose outcomes do not follow a deterministic pattern, but follow an evolution described by probability distributions. For example, a random sample of individuals from a population refers to a sample where every individual has a known probability of being sampled. |
| Statistical significance | Statistical significance is the probability that an effect is not due to just chance alone. It is an integral part of statistical hypothesis testing where it is used as an important value judgment. In statistics, a result is considered significant not because it is important or meaningful, but because it has been predicted as unlikely to have occurred by chance alone. |

17. Inferences About Means

1. In probability and statistics, _____-distribution is a family of continuous probability distributions that arise when estimating the mean of a normally distributed population in situations where the sample size is small and population standard deviation is unknown. It plays a role in a number of widely used statistical analyses, including the _____ -test for assessing the statistical significance of the difference between two sample means, the construction of confidence intervals for the difference between two population means, and in linear regression analysis. The _____-distribution also arises in the Bayesian analysis of data from a normal family.

   a. negative binomial
   b. multivariate normal
   c. beta-binomial
   d. Student's t

2. In physics, _____ is the rate of doing work. It is equivalent to an amount of energy consumed per unit time. In the MKS system, the unit of _____ is the joule per second (J/s), known as the watt in honor of James Watt, the eighteenth-century developer of the steam engine.

   a. Power
   b. Bohr magneton
   c. Bohr model
   d. Boiling point

3. The word _____ entails different meanings and usages relative to how it is conceptually applied. The concrete meaning of the Latin word '_____' is 'wandering' or 'straying'. Unlike an illusion, an _____ or a mistake can sometimes be dispelled through knowledge (knowing that one is looking at a mirage and not at real water does not make the mirage disappear).

   a. 0 to 60 mph
   b. Baculometry
   c. Error
   d. Berkson error model

4. _____ determination is the act of choosing the number of observations or replicates to include in a statistical sample. The _____ is an important feature of any empirical study in which the goal is to make inferences about a population from a sample. In practice, the _____ used in a study is determined based on the expense of data collection, and the need to have sufficient statistical power.

   a. Manhattan Project
   b. Deep sampling
   c. Judgment sample
   d. Sample size

17. Inferences About Means

5. In probability theory, the _____ states that, given certain conditions, the arithmetic mean of a sufficiently large number of iterates of independent random variables, each with a well-defined expected value and well-defined variance, will be approximately normally distributed. That is, suppose that a sample is obtained containing a large number of observations, each observation being randomly generated in a way that does not depend on the values of the other observations, and that the arithmetic average of the observed values is computed. If this procedure is performed many times, the _____ says that the computed values of the average will be distributed according to the normal distribution (commonly known as a 'bell curve').

   a. Covariance
   b. Law of total covariance
   c. Central limit theorem
   d. Law of total expectation

1. d
2. a
3. c
4. d
5. c

You can take the complete Chapter Practice Test

for 17. Inferences About Means
on all key terms, persons, places, and concepts.

Online 99 Cents

http://www.JustTheFacts101.com

Use www.JustTheFacts101.com for all your study needs

including Facts101's online interactive problem solving labs in

chemistry, statistics, mathematics, and more.

CHAPTER OUTLINE: KEY TERMS, PEOPLE, PLACES, CONCEPTS

_____ | Alternative hypothesis

_____ | P-value

_____ | Conditional probability

_____ | Difference

_____ | Error

_____ | Standard error

_____ | Statistical significance

_____ | Level

_____ | Null hypothesis

_____ | Confidence interval

_____ | Regression

_____ | Type

_____ | Type I error

_____ | Type II error

_____ | Hypothesis

_____ | Risk

_____ | Meta-analysis

_____ | Effect size

_____ | Size

18. More About Tests and Intervals

Alternative hypothesis	In statistical hypothesis testing, the alternative hypothesis and the null hypothesis are the two rival hypotheses which are compared by a statistical hypothesis test. An example might be where water quality in a stream has been observed over many years and a test is made of the null hypothesis that there is no change in quality between the first and second halves of the data against the alternative hypothesis that the quality is poorer in the second half of the record. In the case of a scalar parameter, there are four principal types of alternative hypothesis:•Point. Point alternative hypotheses occur when the hypothesis test is framed so that the population distribution under the alternative hypothesis is a fully defined distribution, with no unknown parameters; such hypotheses are usually of no practical interest but are fundamental to theoretical considerations of statistical inference and are the basis of the Neyman-Pearson lemma.•One-tailed directional. A one-tailed directional alternative hypothesis is concerned with the region of rejection for only one tail of the sampling distribution.•Two-tailed directional. A two-tailed directional alternative hypothesis is concerned with both regions of rejection of the sampling distribution.•Non-directional. A non-directional alternative hypothesis is not concerned with either region of rejection, but, rather, it is only concerned that null hypothesis is not true.
P-value	In statistical significance testing, the p-value is the probability of obtaining a test statistic at least as extreme as the one that was actually observed, assuming that the null hypothesis is true. A researcher will often 'reject the null hypothesis' when the p-value turns out to be less than a certain significance level, often 0.05 or 0.01. Such a result indicates that the observed result would be highly unlikely under the null hypothesis. Many common statistical tests, such as chi-squared tests or Student's t-test, produce test statistics which can be interpreted using p-values.
Conditional probability	In probability theory, a conditional probability measures the probability of an event given that another event has occurred. If the events are A and B respectively, this is said to be 'the probability of A given B'. It is commonly denoted by $P(A\backslash B)$, or sometimes $P_B(A)$.
Difference	Difference is a key concept of philosophy, denoting the process or set of properties by which one entity is distinguished from another within a relational field or a given conceptual system. In the Western philosophical system, difference is traditionally viewed as being opposed to identity, following the Principles of Leibniz, and in particular his Law of the Identity of indiscernibles. In structuralist and poststructuralist accounts, however, difference is understood to be constitutive of both meaning and identity.
Error	The word error entails different meanings and usages relative to how it is conceptually applied. The concrete meaning of the Latin word 'error' is 'wandering' or 'straying'. Unlike an illusion, an error or a mistake can sometimes be dispelled through knowledge (knowing that one is looking at a mirage and not at real water does not make the mirage disappear).
Standard error	The standard error is the standard deviation of the sampling distribution of a statistic.

18. More About Tests and Intervals

CHAPTER HIGHLIGHTS & NOTES: KEY TERMS, PEOPLE, PLACES, CONCEPTS

The term may also be used to refer to an estimate of that standard deviation, derived from a particular sample used to compute the estimate.

For example, the sample mean is the usual estimator of a population mean.

Statistical significance	Statistical significance is the probability that an effect is not due to just chance alone. It is an integral part of statistical hypothesis testing where it is used as an important value judgment. In statistics, a result is considered significant not because it is important or meaningful, but because it has been predicted as unlikely to have occurred by chance alone.
Level	In the International System of Quantities, a level is the logarithm of the ratio of a quantity Q to a reference value of that quantity, Q_0. Examples are sound pressure level, sound power level and sound exposure level. In equation form: $L_Q = \log(Q/Q_0)$.
Null hypothesis	In statistical inference of observed data of a scientific experiment, the null hypothesis refers to a general or default position: that there is no relationship between two measured phenomena, or that a potential medical treatment has no effect. Rejecting or disproving the null hypothesis - and thus concluding that there are grounds for believing that there is a relationship between two phenomena or that a potential treatment has a measurable effect - is a central task in the modern practice of science, and gives a precise sense in which a claim is capable of being proven false. In statistical significance, the null hypothesis is often denoted H_0 (read "H-nought" in Britain or 'H-zero' in America), and is generally assumed true until evidence indicates otherwise (e.g., H_0: μ = 500 hours).
Confidence interval	In statistical inference, the concept of a confidence distribution has often been loosely referred to as a distribution function on the parameter space that can represent confidence intervals of all levels for a parameter of interest. Historically, it has typically been constructed by inverting the upper limits of lower sided confidence intervals of all levels, and it was also commonly associated with a fiducial interpretation (fiducial distribution), although it is a purely frequentist concept. A confidence distribution is not a valid probability distribution, but may still be a function useful for making inferences.
Regression	Regression in medicine is a characteristic of diseases to show lighter symptoms without completely disappearing. At a later point, symptoms may return. These symptoms are then called recidive.
Type	In biology, a type is one particular specimen of an organism to which the scientific name of that organism is formally attached. In other words, a type is an example that serves to anchor or centralize the defining features of that particular taxon.

18. More About Tests and Intervals

Type I error

In statistics, a null hypothesis is a statement that the thing being studied produces no effect or makes no difference. An example of a null hypothesis is the statement 'This diet has no effect on people's weight.' Usually an experimenter frames a null hypothesis with the intent of rejecting it: that is, intending to run an experiment which produces data that shows that the thing under study does make a difference.

A type I error is the incorrect rejection of a true null hypothesis.

Type II error

A type II error (or error of the second kind) is the failure to reject a false null hypothesis. With respect to the non-null hypothesis, it represents a false negative. Examples of type II errors would be a blood test failing to detect the disease it was designed to detect, in a patient who really has the disease; a fire breaking out and the fire alarm does not ring or a clinical trial of a medical treatment failing to show that the treatment works when really it does.

When comparing two means, concluding the means were different when in reality they were not different would be a Type I error; concluding the means were not different when in reality they were different would be a Type II error.

Hypothesis

A hypothesis is a proposed explanation for a phenomenon. For a hypothesis to be a scientific hypothesis, the scientific method requires that one can test it. Scientists generally base scientific hypotheses on previous observations that cannot satisfactorily be explained with the available scientific theories.

Risk

Risk is the potential of losing something of value, weighed against the potential to gain something of value. Values (such as physical health, social status, emotional well being or financial wealth) can be gained or lost when taking risk resulting from a given action, activity and/or inaction, foreseen or unforeseen. Risk can also be defined as the intentional interaction with uncertainty.

Meta-analysis

Levels of evidence is a ranking system used in evidence-based practices to describe the strength of the results measured in a clinical trial or research study. The design of the study (such as a case report for an individual patient or a double-blinded randomized controlled trial) and the endpoints measured (such as survival or quality of life) affect the strength of the evidence. Levels of evidence range from I-IV.•Ia - Evidence from Meta-analysis of Randomized Controlled Trials•Ib - Evidence from at least one Randomized Controlled Trial•IIa - Evidence from at least one well designed controlled trial which is not randomized•IIb - Evidence from at least one well designed experimental trial•III - Evidence from case, correlation, and comparative studies.•IV - Evidence from a panel of experts.

Effect size

In statistics, an effect size is a measure of the strength of a phenomenon . An effect size calculated from data is a descriptive statistic that conveys the estimated magnitude of a relationship without making any statement about whether the apparent relationship in the data reflects a true relationship in the population.

Size	In statistics, the size of a statistical test is the maximum of the probabilities of a type I error, i.e. of the probabilities of falsely rejecting the null hypothesis. In the case of a simple null hypothesis the size is the only possible probability of a type I error. The size of a test is denoted by the Greek letter a (alpha).

CHAPTER QUIZ: KEY TERMS, PEOPLE, PLACES, CONCEPTS

1. In probability theory, a _____ measures the probability of an event given that another event has occurred. If the events are A and B respectively, this is said to be 'the probability of A given B'. It is commonly denoted by P(A\B), or sometimes $P_B(A)$.

   a. Conditional probability
   b. B-convex space
   c. Bean machine
   d. Chain rule

2. In statistical hypothesis testing, the _____ and the null hypothesis are the two rival hypotheses which are compared by a statistical hypothesis test. An example might be where water quality in a stream has been observed over many years and a test is made of the null hypothesis that there is no change in quality between the first and second halves of the data against the _____ that the quality is poorer in the second half of the record.

   In the case of a scalar parameter, there are four principal types of _____:•Point. Point alternative hypotheses occur when the hypothesis test is framed so that the population distribution under the _____ is a fully defined distribution, with no unknown parameters; such hypotheses are usually of no practical interest but are fundamental to theoretical considerations of statistical inference and are the basis of the Neyman-Pearson lemma.•One-tailed directional. A one-tailed directional _____ is concerned with the region of rejection for only one tail of the sampling distribution.•Two-tailed directional. A two-tailed directional _____ is concerned with both regions of rejection of the sampling distribution.•Non-directional. A non-directional _____ is not concerned with either region of rejection, but, rather, it is only concerned that null hypothesis is not true.

   a. Alternative hypothesis
   b. Credal set
   c. Causality
   d. Causal decision theory

3. . _____ is a key concept of philosophy, denoting the process or set of properties by which one entity is distinguished from another within a relational field or a given conceptual system. In the Western philosophical system, _____ is traditionally viewed as being opposed to identity, following the Principles of Leibniz, and in particular his Law of the Identity of indiscernibles.

In structuralist and poststructuralist accounts, however, _____ is understood to be constitutive of both meaning and identity.

    a. Belief revision
    b. Difference
    c. Canon
    d. Ceqli

4. In statistical inference, the concept of a confidence distribution has often been loosely referred to as a distribution function on the parameter space that can represent _____s of all levels for a parameter of interest. Historically, it has typically been constructed by inverting the upper limits of lower sided _____s of all levels, and it was also commonly associated with a fiducial interpretation (fiducial distribution), although it is a purely frequentist concept. A confidence distribution is not a valid probability distribution, but may still be a function useful for making inferences.

    a. Statistical inference
    b. Confidence interval
    c. Fuzzy-trace theory
    d. Dutch book

5. In statistical inference of observed data of a scientific experiment, the _____ refers to a general or default position: that there is no relationship between two measured phenomena, or that a potential medical treatment has no effect. Rejecting or disproving the _____ - and thus concluding that there are grounds for believing that there is a relationship between two phenomena or that a potential treatment has a measurable effect - is a central task in the modern practice of science, and gives a precise sense in which a claim is capable of being proven false.

In statistical significance, the _____ is often denoted H_0 (read "H-nought" in Britain or 'H-zero' in America), and is generally assumed true until evidence indicates otherwise (e.g., H_0: $\mu = 500$ hours).

    a. Null hypothesis
    b. Generalized p-value
    c. Minimum chi-square estimation
    d. Covariance

1. a
2. a
3. b
4. b
5. a

You can take the complete Chapter Practice Test

for 18. More About Tests and Intervals
on all key terms, persons, places, and concepts.

Online 99 Cents

http://www.JustTheFacts101.com

Use www.JustTheFacts101.com for all your study needs

including Facts101's online interactive problem solving labs in

chemistry, statistics, mathematics, and more.

19. Comparing Groups

CHAPTER OUTLINE: KEY TERMS, PEOPLE, PLACES, CONCEPTS

_____ Difference

_____ Error

_____ Sample

_____ Standard error

_____ Theorem

_____ Deviation

_____ Sampling

_____ Sampling distribution

_____ Standard deviation

_____ Variance

_____ Pythagorean theorem

_____ Sample size

_____ Chi-square test

_____ Conditional probability

_____ Distribution

_____ Probability

_____ Regression

_____ Test

_____ Power

_____ Z-test

_____ Mean

19. Comparing Groups

	Complement
	Condition
	Randomization
	Degrees of freedom
	Hypothesis
	T-test
	Confidence interval

CHAPTER HIGHLIGHTS & NOTES: KEY TERMS, PEOPLE, PLACES, CONCEPTS

Difference

Difference is a key concept of philosophy, denoting the process or set of properties by which one entity is distinguished from another within a relational field or a given conceptual system. In the Western philosophical system, difference is traditionally viewed as being opposed to identity, following the Principles of Leibniz, and in particular his Law of the Identity of indiscernibles. In structuralist and poststructuralist accounts, however, difference is understood to be constitutive of both meaning and identity.

Error

The word error entails different meanings and usages relative to how it is conceptually applied. The concrete meaning of the Latin word 'error' is 'wandering' or 'straying'. Unlike an illusion, an error or a mistake can sometimes be dispelled through knowledge (knowing that one is looking at a mirage and not at real water does not make the mirage disappear).

Sample

In statistics and quantitative research methodology, a data sample is a set of data collected and/or selected from a statistical population by a defined procedure.

Standard error

The standard error is the standard deviation of the sampling distribution of a statistic. The term may also be used to refer to an estimate of that standard deviation, derived from a particular sample used to compute the estimate.

For example, the sample mean is the usual estimator of a population mean.

Theorem	In mathematics, a theorem is a statement that has been proven on the basis of previously established statements, such as other theorems--and generally accepted statements, such as axioms. The proof of a mathematical theorem is a logical argument for the theorem statement given in accord with the rules of a deductive system. The proof of a theorem is often interpreted as justification of the truth of the theorem statement.
Deviation	In mathematics and statistics, deviation is a measure of difference between the observed value of a variable and some other value, often that variable's mean. The sign of the deviation reports the direction of that difference (the deviation is positive when the observed value exceeds the reference value). The magnitude of the value indicates the size of the difference.
Sampling	In statistics, quality assurance, & survey methodology, sampling is concerned with the selection of a subset of individuals from within a statistical population to estimate characteristics of the whole population. Each observation measures one or more properties (such as weight, location, color) of observable bodies distinguished as independent objects or individuals. In survey sampling, weights can be applied to the data to adjust for the sample design, particularly stratified sampling.
Sampling distribution	In statistics, a sampling distribution or finite-sample distribution is the probability distribution of a given statistic based on a random sample. Sampling distributions are important in statistics because they provide a major simplification on the route to statistical inference. More specifically, they allow analytical considerations to be based on the sampling distribution of a statistic, rather than on the joint probability distribution of all the individual sample values.
Standard deviation	In statistics and probability theory, the standard deviation shows how much variation or dispersion from the average exists. A low standard deviation indicates that the data points tend to be very close to the mean (also called expected value); a high standard deviation indicates that the data points are spread out over a large range of values. The standard deviation of a random variable, statistical population, data set, or probability distribution is the square root of its variance.
Variance	In probability theory and statistics, variance measures how far a set of numbers is spread out. (A variance of zero indicates that all the values are identical). Variance is always non-negative: A small variance indicates that the data points tend to be very close to the mean (expected value) and hence to each other, while a high variance indicates that the data points are very spread out from the mean and from each other.
Pythagorean theorem	In mathematics, the Pythagorean theorem--or Pythagoras' theorem--is a relation in Euclidean geometry among the three sides of a right triangle. It states that the square of the hypotenuse (the side opposite the right angle) is equal to the sum of the squares of the other two sides. The theorem can be written as an equation relating the lengths of the sides a, b and c, often called the Pythagorean equation: $a^2 + b^2 = c^2$

19. Comparing Groups

Sample size	Sample size determination is the act of choosing the number of observations or replicates to include in a statistical sample. The sample size is an important feature of any empirical study in which the goal is to make inferences about a population from a sample. In practice, the sample size used in a study is determined based on the expense of data collection, and the need to have sufficient statistical power.
Chi-square test	A chi-squared test, also referred to as chi-square test or χ^2 test, is any statistical hypothesis test in which the sampling distribution of the test statistic is a chi-squared distribution when the null hypothesis is true. Also considered a chi-squared test is a test in which this is asymptotically true, meaning that the sampling distribution (if the null hypothesis is true) can be made to approximate a chi-squared distribution as closely as desired by making the sample size large enough. Some examples of chi-squared tests where the chi-squared distribution is only approximately valid:•Pearson's chi-squared test, also known as the chi-squared goodness-of-fit test or chi-squared test for independence.
Conditional probability	In probability theory, a conditional probability measures the probability of an event given that another event has occurred. If the events are A and B respectively, this is said to be 'the probability of A given B'. It is commonly denoted by P(A\B), or sometimes $P_B(A)$.
Distribution	In algebra and number theory, a distribution is a function on a system of finite sets into an abelian group which is analogous to an integral: it is thus the algebraic analogue of a distribution in the sense of generalised function. The original examples of distributions occur, unnamed, as functions f on Q/Z satisfying $$\sum_{r=0}^{N-1} \phi\left(x + \frac{r}{N}\right) = \phi(Nx) \ .$$ We shall call these ordinary distributions. They also occur in p-adic integration theory in Iwasawa theory.
Probability	Probability is a measure of the likeliness that an event will occur. Probability is used to quantify an attitude of mind towards some proposition of whose truth we are not certain. The proposition of interest is usually of the form 'Will a specific event occur?' The attitude of mind is of the form 'How certain are we that the event will occur?' The certainty we adopt can be described in terms of a numerical measure and this number, between 0 and 1 (where 0 indicates impossibility and 1 indicates certainty), we call probability.
Regression	Regression in medicine is a characteristic of diseases to show lighter symptoms without completely disappearing. At a later point, symptoms may return.

Test	A test or examination is an assessment intended to measure a test-taker's knowledge, skill, aptitude, physical fitness, or classification in many other topics . A test may be administered orally, on paper, on a computer, or in a confined area that requires a test taker to physically perform a set of skills. Tests vary in style, rigor and requirements.
Power	In physics, power is the rate of doing work. It is equivalent to an amount of energy consumed per unit time. In the MKS system, the unit of power is the joule per second (J/s), known as the watt in honor of James Watt, the eighteenth-century developer of the steam engine.
Z-test	A Z-test is any statistical test for which the distribution of the test statistic under the null hypothesis can be approximated by a normal distribution. Because of the central limit theorem, many test statistics are approximately normally distributed for large samples. For each significance level, the Z-test has a single critical value (for example, 1.96 for 5% two tailed) which makes it more convenient than the Student's t-test which has separate critical values for each sample size.
Mean	In probability and statistics, mean and expected value are used synonymously to refer to one measure of the central tendency either of a probability distribution or of the random variable characterized by that distribution. In the case of a discrete probability distribution of a random variable X, the mean is equal to the sum over every possible value weighted by the probability of that value; that is, it is computed by taking the product of each possible value x of X and its probability P(x), and then adding all these products together, giving $$\mu = \sum x P(x)$$
Complement	In set theory, a complement of a set A refers to things not in A. The relative complement of A with respect to a set B is the set of elements in B but not in A. When all sets under consideration are considered to be subsets of a given set U, the absolute complement of A is the set of all elements in U but not in A.
Condition	Comprehensive treatment of the word 'condition' requires emphasizing that it is ambiguous in the sense of having multiple normal meanings and that its meanings are often vague in the sense of admitting borderline cases. According to the 2007 American Philosophy: an Encyclopedia, in one widely used sense, conditions are or resemble qualities, properties, features, characteristics, or attributes. In these senses, a condition is often denoted by a nominalization of a grammatical predicate: 'being equilateral' is a nominalization of the predicate 'is equilateral'.
Randomization	Randomization is the process of making something random; this means: Randomization is not haphazard.

19. Comparing Groups

Instead, a random process is a sequence of random variables describing a process whose outcomes do not follow a deterministic pattern, but follow an evolution described by probability distributions. For example, a random sample of individuals from a population refers to a sample where every individual has a known probability of being sampled.

Degrees of freedom	In many scientific fields, the degrees of freedom of a system is the number of parameters of the system that may vary independently. For example, the position of a figure in the plane has three degrees of freedom: its orientation and the two coordinates of any fixed point of the figure. In mathematics, this notion is formalized as the dimension of a manifold or an algebraic variety.
Hypothesis	A hypothesis is a proposed explanation for a phenomenon. For a hypothesis to be a scientific hypothesis, the scientific method requires that one can test it. Scientists generally base scientific hypotheses on previous observations that cannot satisfactorily be explained with the available scientific theories.
T-test	A t-test is any statistical hypothesis test in which the test statistic follows a Student's t distribution if the null hypothesis is supported. It can be used to determine if two sets of data are significantly different from each other, and is most commonly applied when the test statistic would follow a normal distribution if the value of a scaling term in the test statistic were known. When the scaling term is unknown and is replaced by an estimate based on the data, the test statistic (under certain conditions) follows a Student's t distribution.
Confidence interval	In statistical inference, the concept of a confidence distribution has often been loosely referred to as a distribution function on the parameter space that can represent confidence intervals of all levels for a parameter of interest. Historically, it has typically been constructed by inverting the upper limits of lower sided confidence intervals of all levels, and it was also commonly associated with a fiducial interpretation (fiducial distribution), although it is a purely frequentist concept. A confidence distribution is not a valid probability distribution, but may still be a function useful for making inferences.

1. In statistics, a _____ or finite-sample distribution is the probability distribution of a given statistic based on a random sample. _____s are important in statistics because they provide a major simplification on the route to statistical inference. More specifically, they allow analytical considerations to be based on the _____ of a statistic, rather than on the joint probability distribution of all the individual sample values.

    a. Fisher transformation
    b. L-statistic
    c. Sampling distribution
    d. Pivotal quantity

2. _____ in medicine is a characteristic of diseases to show lighter symptoms without completely disappearing. At a later point, symptoms may return. These symptoms are then called recidive.

    a. 1947 New York City smallpox outbreak
    b. 1993 Four Corners hantavirus outbreak
    c. Regression
    d. 2012 Middle East respiratory syndrome coronavirus outbreak

3. In statistics and quantitative research methodology, a data _____ is a set of data collected and/or selected from a statistical population by a defined procedure.

    a. Correct sampling
    b. Deep sampling
    c. Sample
    d. Lot quality assurance sampling

4. A _____ is a proposed explanation for a phenomenon. For a _____ to be a scientific _____, the scientific method requires that one can test it. Scientists generally base scientific hypotheses on previous observations that cannot satisfactorily be explained with the available scientific theories.

    a. Manhattan Project
    b. Cohort
    c. Hypothesis
    d. Cost-of-living index

5. In probability theory, a _____ measures the probability of an event given that another event has occurred. If the events are A and B respectively, this is said to be 'the probability of A given B'. It is commonly denoted by $P(A\backslash B)$, or sometimes $P_B(A)$.

    a. Conditional probability
    b. B-convex space
    c. Bean machine
    d. Chain rule

1. c
2. c
3. c
4. c
5. a

You can take the complete Chapter Practice Test

for 19. Comparing Groups
on all key terms, persons, places, and concepts.

Online 99 Cents

http://www.JustTheFacts101.com

Use www.JustTheFacts101.com for all your study needs

including Facts101's online interactive problem solving labs in

chemistry, statistics, mathematics, and more.

20. Paired Samples and Blocks

Sample

Confidence interval

Mean

T-test

Blocking

Marginal distribution

Matching

Distribution

Effect size

Size

Condition

Pythagorean theorem

Theorem

Degrees of freedom

Independence

20. Paired Samples and Blocks

Sample	In statistics and quantitative research methodology, a data sample is a set of data collected and/or selected from a statistical population by a defined procedure.
Confidence interval	In statistical inference, the concept of a confidence distribution has often been loosely referred to as a distribution function on the parameter space that can represent confidence intervals of all levels for a parameter of interest. Historically, it has typically been constructed by inverting the upper limits of lower sided confidence intervals of all levels, and it was also commonly associated with a fiducial interpretation (fiducial distribution), although it is a purely frequentist concept. A confidence distribution is not a valid probability distribution, but may still be a function useful for making inferences.
Mean	In probability and statistics, mean and expected value are used synonymously to refer to one measure of the central tendency either of a probability distribution or of the random variable characterized by that distribution. In the case of a discrete probability distribution of a random variable X, the mean is equal to the sum over every possible value weighted by the probability of that value; that is, it is computed by taking the product of each possible value x of X and its probability P(x), and then adding all these products together, giving $$\mu = \sum x P(x)$$.
T-test	A t-test is any statistical hypothesis test in which the test statistic follows a Student's t distribution if the null hypothesis is supported. It can be used to determine if two sets of data are significantly different from each other, and is most commonly applied when the test statistic would follow a normal distribution if the value of a scaling term in the test statistic were known. When the scaling term is unknown and is replaced by an estimate based on the data, the test statistic (under certain conditions) follows a Student's t distribution.
Blocking	In the statistical theory of the design of experiments, blocking is the arranging of experimental units in groups that are similar to one another. For example, an experiment is designed to test a new drug on patients. There are two levels of the treatment, drug, and placebo, administered to male and female patients in a double blind trial.
Marginal distribution	In probability theory and statistics, the marginal distribution of a subset of a collection of random variables is the probability distribution of the variables contained in the subset. It gives the probabilities of various values of the variables in the subset without reference to the values of the other variables. This contrasts with a conditional distribution, which gives the probabilities contingent upon the values of the other variables.
Matching	In the mathematical discipline of graph theory, a matching or independent edge set in a graph is a set of edges without common vertices. It may also be an entire graph consisting of edges without common vertices.

20. Paired Samples and Blocks

Distribution	In algebra and number theory, a distribution is a function on a system of finite sets into an abelian group which is analogous to an integral: it is thus the algebraic analogue of a distribution in the sense of generalised function.

The original examples of distributions occur, unnamed, as functions f on Q/Z satisfying $$\sum_{r=0}^{N-1} \phi\left(x + \frac{r}{N}\right) = \phi(Nx) \ .$$

We shall call these ordinary distributions. They also occur in p-adic integration theory in Iwasawa theory. |
| Effect size | In statistics, an effect size is a measure of the strength of a phenomenon . An effect size calculated from data is a descriptive statistic that conveys the estimated magnitude of a relationship without making any statement about whether the apparent relationship in the data reflects a true relationship in the population. In that way, effect sizes complement inferential statistics such as p-values. |
| Size | In statistics, the size of a statistical test is the maximum of the probabilities of a type I error, i.e. of the probabilities of falsely rejecting the null hypothesis. In the case of a simple null hypothesis the size is the only possible probability of a type I error. The size of a test is denoted by the Greek letter a (alpha). |
| Condition | Comprehensive treatment of the word 'condition' requires emphasizing that it is ambiguous in the sense of having multiple normal meanings and that its meanings are often vague in the sense of admitting borderline cases.

According to the 2007 American Philosophy: an Encyclopedia, in one widely used sense, conditions are or resemble qualities, properties, features, characteristics, or attributes. In these senses, a condition is often denoted by a nominalization of a grammatical predicate: 'being equilateral' is a nominalization of the predicate 'is equilateral'. |
| Pythagorean theorem | In mathematics, the Pythagorean theorem--or Pythagoras' theorem--is a relation in Euclidean geometry among the three sides of a right triangle. It states that the square of the hypotenuse (the side opposite the right angle) is equal to the sum of the squares of the other two sides. The theorem can be written as an equation relating the lengths of the sides a, b and c, often called the Pythagorean equation: $a^2 + b^2 = c^2$

where c represents the length of the hypotenuse, and a and b represent the lengths of the other two sides. |

20. Paired Samples and Blocks

Theorem	In mathematics, a theorem is a statement that has been proven on the basis of previously established statements, such as other theorems--and generally accepted statements, such as axioms. The proof of a mathematical theorem is a logical argument for the theorem statement given in accord with the rules of a deductive system. The proof of a theorem is often interpreted as justification of the truth of the theorem statement.
Degrees of freedom	In many scientific fields, the degrees of freedom of a system is the number of parameters of the system that may vary independently. For example, the position of a figure in the plane has three degrees of freedom: its orientation and the two coordinates of any fixed point of the figure. In mathematics, this notion is formalized as the dimension of a manifold or an algebraic variety.
Independence	In probability theory, to say that two events are independent means that the occurrence of one does not affect the probability of the other. Similarly, two random variables are independent if the realization of one does not affect the probability distribution of the other. The concept of independence extends to dealing with collections of more than two events or random variables.

1. In the mathematical discipline of graph theory, a _____ or independent edge set in a graph is a set of edges without common vertices. It may also be an entire graph consisting of edges without common vertices.

   a. Matching
   b. Branch and bound
   c. Branch and cut
   d. Branch and price

2. . In probability theory, to say that two events are independent means that the occurrence of one does not affect the probability of the other. Similarly, two random variables are independent if the realization of one does not affect the probability distribution of the other.

   The concept of _____ extends to dealing with collections of more than two events or random variables.

   a. Bayesian programming
   b. B-convex space
   c. Independence

20. Paired Samples and Blocks

3. In statistics, the _____ of a statistical test is the maximum of the probabilities of a type I error, i.e. of the probabilities of falsely rejecting the null hypothesis. In the case of a simple null hypothesis the _____ is the only possible probability of a type I error. The _____ of a test is denoted by the Greek letter a (alpha).

   a. Deviance
   b. Generalized p-value
   c. Minimum chi-square estimation
   d. Size

4. In statistics, an _____ is a measure of the strength of a phenomenon . An _____ calculated from data is a descriptive statistic that conveys the estimated magnitude of a relationship without making any statement about whether the apparent relationship in the data reflects a true relationship in the population. In that way, _____s complement inferential statistics such as p-values.

   a. Effect size
   b. Summary statistic
   c. Central tendency
   d. Circular error probable

5. In probability and statistics, _____ and expected value are used synonymously to refer to one measure of the central tendency either of a probability distribution or of the random variable characterized by that distribution. In the case of a discrete probability distribution of a random variable X, the _____ is equal to the sum over every possible value weighted by the probability of that value; that is, it is computed by taking the product of each possible value x of X and its probability P(x), and then adding all these products together, giving

$$\mu = \sum x P(x)$$

   a. Bias of an estimator
   b. Summary statistic
   c. Central tendency
   d. Mean

1. a
2. c
3. d
4. a
5. d

You can take the complete Chapter Practice Test

for 20. Paired Samples and Blocks
on all key terms, persons, places, and concepts.

Online 99 Cents

http://www.JustTheFacts101.com

Use www.JustTheFacts101.com for all your study needs

including Facts101's online interactive problem solving labs in

chemistry, statistics, mathematics, and more.

21. Comparing Counts

CHAPTER OUTLINE: KEY TERMS, PEOPLE, PLACES, CONCEPTS

_____ Z-test

_____ Condition

_____ Sample size

_____ Correlation

_____ Statistic

_____ Theorem

_____ Alternative hypothesis

_____ Expected value

_____ Hypothesis

_____ Process

_____ Value

_____ Conditional probability

_____ Probability

_____ Test

_____ Null hypothesis

_____ Homogeneity

_____ Regression

_____ Independence

_____ Residual

_____ Causation

_____ Dependent variables

21. Comparing Counts

Z-test	A Z-test is any statistical test for which the distribution of the test statistic under the null hypothesis can be approximated by a normal distribution. Because of the central limit theorem, many test statistics are approximately normally distributed for large samples. For each significance level, the Z-test has a single critical value (for example, 1.96 for 5% two tailed) which makes it more convenient than the Student's t-test which has separate critical values for each sample size.
Condition	Comprehensive treatment of the word 'condition' requires emphasizing that it is ambiguous in the sense of having multiple normal meanings and that its meanings are often vague in the sense of admitting borderline cases.

According to the 2007 American Philosophy: an Encyclopedia, in one widely used sense, conditions are or resemble qualities, properties, features, characteristics, or attributes. In these senses, a condition is often denoted by a nominalization of a grammatical predicate: 'being equilateral' is a nominalization of the predicate 'is equilateral'. |
| Sample size | Sample size determination is the act of choosing the number of observations or replicates to include in a statistical sample. The sample size is an important feature of any empirical study in which the goal is to make inferences about a population from a sample. In practice, the sample size used in a study is determined based on the expense of data collection, and the need to have sufficient statistical power. |
| Correlation | In statistics, dependence is any statistical relationship between two random variables or two sets of data. Correlation refers to any of a broad class of statistical relationships involving dependence.

Familiar examples of dependent phenomena include the correlation between the physical statures of parents and their offspring, and the correlation between the demand for a product and its price. |
| Statistic | A statistic is a single measure of some attribute of a sample (e.g., its arithmetic mean value). It is calculated by applying a function (statistical algorithm) to the values of the items of the sample, which are known together as a set of data.

More formally, statistical theory defines a statistic as a function of a sample where the function itself is independent of the sample's distribution; that is, the function can be stated before realization of the data. |
| Theorem | In mathematics, a theorem is a statement that has been proven on the basis of previously established statements, such as other theorems--and generally accepted statements, such as axioms. The proof of a mathematical theorem is a logical argument for the theorem statement given in accord with the rules of a deductive system. The proof of a theorem is often interpreted as justification of the truth of the theorem statement. |

21. Comparing Counts

Alternative hypothesis	In statistical hypothesis testing, the alternative hypothesis and the null hypothesis are the two rival hypotheses which are compared by a statistical hypothesis test. An example might be where water quality in a stream has been observed over many years and a test is made of the null hypothesis that there is no change in quality between the first and second halves of the data against the alternative hypothesis that the quality is poorer in the second half of the record. In the case of a scalar parameter, there are four principal types of alternative hypothesis:•Point. Point alternative hypotheses occur when the hypothesis test is framed so that the population distribution under the alternative hypothesis is a fully defined distribution, with no unknown parameters; such hypotheses are usually of no practical interest but are fundamental to theoretical considerations of statistical inference and are the basis of the Neyman-Pearson lemma.•One-tailed directional. A one-tailed directional alternative hypothesis is concerned with the region of rejection for only one tail of the sampling distribution.•Two-tailed directional. A two-tailed directional alternative hypothesis is concerned with both regions of rejection of the sampling distribution.•Non-directional. A non-directional alternative hypothesis is not concerned with either region of rejection, but, rather, it is only concerned that null hypothesis is not true.
Expected value	In probability theory, the expected value refers, intuitively, to the value of a random variable one would 'expect' to find if one could repeat the random variable process an infinite number of times and take the average of the values obtained. More formally, the expected value is a weighted average of all possible values. In other words, each possible value that the random variable can assume is multiplied by its assigned weight, and the resulting products are then added together to find the expected value.
Hypothesis	A hypothesis is a proposed explanation for a phenomenon. For a hypothesis to be a scientific hypothesis, the scientific method requires that one can test it. Scientists generally base scientific hypotheses on previous observations that cannot satisfactorily be explained with the available scientific theories.
Process	The process of science is the scientific method. This is the process of constructing an accurate, reliable, repeatable model of the real world, by scientists collectively working towards this goal over time. The scientific method is the complex process of 'doing science', that is, being expert in the content area and the scientific method.
Value	In ethics, value denotes something's degree of importance, with the aim of determining what action or life is best to do or live, or at least attempt to describe the value of different actions (Axiology). It may be described as treating actions themselves as abstract objects, putting value to them.

21. Comparing Counts

Conditional probability	In probability theory, a conditional probability measures the probability of an event given that another event has occurred. If the events are A and B respectively, this is said to be 'the probability of A given B'. It is commonly denoted by $P(A\backslash B)$, or sometimes $P_B(A)$.
Probability	Probability is a measure of the likeliness that an event will occur.
	Probability is used to quantify an attitude of mind towards some proposition of whose truth we are not certain. The proposition of interest is usually of the form 'Will a specific event occur?' The attitude of mind is of the form 'How certain are we that the event will occur?' The certainty we adopt can be described in terms of a numerical measure and this number, between 0 and 1 (where 0 indicates impossibility and 1 indicates certainty), we call probability.
Test	A test or examination is an assessment intended to measure a test-taker's knowledge, skill, aptitude, physical fitness, or classification in many other topics . A test may be administered orally, on paper, on a computer, or in a confined area that requires a test taker to physically perform a set of skills. Tests vary in style, rigor and requirements.
Null hypothesis	In statistical inference of observed data of a scientific experiment, the null hypothesis refers to a general or default position: that there is no relationship between two measured phenomena, or that a potential medical treatment has no effect. Rejecting or disproving the null hypothesis - and thus concluding that there are grounds for believing that there is a relationship between two phenomena or that a potential treatment has a measurable effect - is a central task in the modern practice of science, and gives a precise sense in which a claim is capable of being proven false.
	In statistical significance, the null hypothesis is often denoted H_0 (read "H-nought" in Britain or 'H-zero' in America), and is generally assumed true until evidence indicates otherwise (e.g., H_0: $\mu = 500$ hours).
Homogeneity	In statistics, homogeneity and its opposite, heterogeneity, arise in describing the properties of a dataset, or several datasets. They relate to the validity of the often convenient assumption that the statistical properties of any one part of an overall dataset are the same as any other part. In meta-analysis, which combines the data from several studies, homogeneity measures the differences or similarities between the several studies .
Regression	Regression in medicine is a characteristic of diseases to show lighter symptoms without completely disappearing. At a later point, symptoms may return. These symptoms are then called recidive.
Independence	In probability theory, to say that two events are independent means that the occurrence of one does not affect the probability of the other. Similarly, two random variables are independent if the realization of one does not affect the probability distribution of the other.

21. Comparing Counts

Residual	Loosely speaking, a residual is the error in a result. To be precise, suppose we want to find x such that $f(x) = b.$
	Given an approximation x_0 of x, the residual is $b - f(x_0)$
	whereas the error is $x_0 - x.$
	If we do not know x, we cannot compute the error but we can compute the residual.
Causation	Causation is the 'causal relationship between conduct and result'. That is to say that causation provides a means of connecting conduct with a resulting effect, typically an injury. In criminal law, it is defined as the actus reus (an action) from which the specific injury or other effect arose and is combined with mens rea (a state of mind) to comprise the elements of guilt.
Dependent variables	Variables used in an experiment or modelling can be divided into three types: 'dependent variable', 'independent variable', or other. The 'dependent variable' represents the output or effect, or is tested to see if it is the effect. The 'independent variables' represent the inputs or causes, or are tested to see if they are the cause.

1. . In statistical hypothesis testing, the _____ and the null hypothesis are the two rival hypotheses which are compared by a statistical hypothesis test. An example might be where water quality in a stream has been observed over many years and a test is made of the null hypothesis that there is no change in quality between the first and second halves of the data against the _____ that the quality is poorer in the second half of the record.

In the case of a scalar parameter, there are four principal types of _____:•Point. Point alternative hypotheses occur when the hypothesis test is framed so that the population distribution under the _____ is a fully defined distribution, with no unknown parameters; such hypotheses are usually of no practical interest but are fundamental to theoretical considerations of statistical inference and are the basis of the Neyman-Pearson lemma.•One-tailed directional. A one-tailed directional _____ is concerned with the region of rejection for only one tail of the sampling distribution.•Two-tailed directional. A two-tailed directional _____ is concerned with both regions of rejection of the sampling distribution.•Non-directional. A non-directional _____ is not concerned with either region of rejection, but, rather, it is only concerned that null hypothesis is not true.

a. Bayesian inference
b. Alternative hypothesis

c. Causality

d. Causal decision theory

2. A _____ is any statistical test for which the distribution of the test statistic under the null hypothesis can be approximated by a normal distribution. Because of the central limit theorem, many test statistics are approximately normally distributed for large samples. For each significance level, the _____ has a single critical value (for example, 1.96 for 5% two tailed) which makes it more convenient than the Student's t-test which has separate critical values for each sample size.

    a. Normal probability plot

    b. Rankit

    c. Z-test

    d. Covariance

3. Variables used in an experiment or modelling can be divided into three types: '_____(es)', 'in_____(es)', or other. The '_____(es)' represents the output or effect, or is tested to see if it is the effect. The 'in_____' represent the inputs or causes, or are tested to see if they are the cause.

    a. Manhattan Project

    b. Dependent variables

    c. Butterfly effect

    d. Causal chain

4. Comprehensive treatment of the word '_____' requires emphasizing that it is ambiguous in the sense of having multiple normal meanings and that its meanings are often vague in the sense of admitting borderline cases.

    According to the 2007 American Philosophy: an Encyclopedia, in one widely used sense, _____s are or resemble qualities, properties, features, characteristics, or attributes. In these senses, a _____ is often denoted by a nominalization of a grammatical predicate: 'being equilateral' is a nominalization of the predicate 'is equilateral'.

    a. Belief revision

    b. Boolean network

    c. Condition

    d. Ceqli

5. . In statistics, dependence is any statistical relationship between two random variables or two sets of data. _____ refers to any of a broad class of statistical relationships involving dependence.

    Familiar examples of dependent phenomena include the _____ between the physical statures of parents and their offspring, and the _____ between the demand for a product and its price.

    a. Dimensionless quantity

    b. Correlation

    c. Beale number

1. b
2. c
3. b
4. c
5. b

You can take the complete Chapter Practice Test

for 21. Comparing Counts
on all key terms, persons, places, and concepts.

Online 99 Cents

http://www.JustTheFacts101.com

Use www.JustTheFacts101.com for all your study needs

including Facts101's online interactive problem solving labs in

chemistry, statistics, mathematics, and more.

22. Inferences for Regression

CHAPTER OUTLINE: KEY TERMS, PEOPLE, PLACES, CONCEPTS

Linear regression

Regression

Least squares

Population

Sample

Slope

Condition

Inference

Residual

Standard deviation

Linear model

Deviation

Interquartile range

Random variable

Range

Degrees of freedom

Error

Sampling distribution

Standard error

T-statistic

Power

_____ Hypothesis

_____ Hypothesis test

_____ Mean

_____ T-test

_____ Logistic regression

_____ Extrapolation

_____ Regression analysis

_____ F-distribution

_____ F-test

_____ Statistical significance

_____ Confidence interval

_____ Contrast

_____ Experiment

_____ Complement

_____ One-way ANOVA

_____ Bonferroni method

_____ Multiple comparisons

_____ Theorem

_____ Ordinary least squares

_____ Partial regression plot

_____ Coefficient

22. Inferences for Regression

	Conditional probability
	Probability
	Infant mortality
	Independence

CHAPTER HIGHLIGHTS & NOTES: KEY TERMS, PEOPLE, PLACES, CONCEPTS

Linear regression	In statistics, linear regression is an approach for modeling the relationship between a scalar dependent variable y and one or more explanatory variables denoted X. The case of one explanatory variable is called simple linear regression. For more than one explanatory variable, the process is called multiple linear regression. (This term should be distinguished from multivariate linear regression, where multiple correlated dependent variables are predicted, rather than a single scalar variable).
Regression	Regression in medicine is a characteristic of diseases to show lighter symptoms without completely disappearing. At a later point, symptoms may return. These symptoms are then called recidive.
Least squares	The method of least squares is a standard approach to the approximate solution of overdetermined systems, i.e., sets of equations in which there are more equations than unknowns. 'Least squares' means that the overall solution minimizes the sum of the squares of the errors made in the results of every single equation. The most important application is in data fitting.
Population	A statistical population is a set of individuals or objects of interest. A subset of a population is called a subpopulation. If different subpopulations have different properties, so the overall population is heterogeneous, the properties and response of the overall population can often be better understood if it is first separated into distinct subpopulations. For instance, a particular medicine may have different effects on different subpopulations, and these effects may be obscured or dismissed if such special subpopulations are not identified and examined in isolation.

22. Inferences for Regression

Sample	In statistics and quantitative research methodology, a data sample is a set of data collected and/or selected from a statistical population by a defined procedure.
Slope	In mathematics, the slope or gradient of a line is a number that describes both the direction and the steepness of the line. Slope is often denoted by the letter m. •The direction of a line is either increasing, decreasing, horizontal or vertical.•A line is increasing if it goes up from left to right.
Condition	Comprehensive treatment of the word 'condition' requires emphasizing that it is ambiguous in the sense of having multiple normal meanings and that its meanings are often vague in the sense of admitting borderline cases. According to the 2007 American Philosophy: an Encyclopedia, in one widely used sense, conditions are or resemble qualities, properties, features, characteristics, or attributes. In these senses, a condition is often denoted by a nominalization of a grammatical predicate: 'being equilateral' is a nominalization of the predicate 'is equilateral'.
Inference	Inference is the act or process of deriving logical conclusions from premises known or assumed to be true. The conclusion drawn is also called an idiomatic. The laws of valid inference are studied in the field of logic.
Residual	Loosely speaking, a residual is the error in a result. To be precise, suppose we want to find x such that $f(x) = b.$ Given an approximation x_0 of x, the residual is $b - f(x_0)$ whereas the error is $x_0 - x.$ If we do not know x, we cannot compute the error but we can compute the residual.
Standard deviation	In statistics and probability theory, the standard deviation shows how much variation or dispersion from the average exists. A low standard deviation indicates that the data points tend to be very close to the mean (also called expected value); a high standard deviation indicates that the data points are spread out over a large range of values. The standard deviation of a random variable, statistical population, data set, or probability distribution is the square root of its variance.
Linear model	In statistics, the term linear model is used in different ways according to the context. The most common occurrence is in connection with regression models and the term is often taken as synonymous with linear regression model.

22. Inferences for Regression

Deviation	In mathematics and statistics, deviation is a measure of difference between the observed value of a variable and some other value, often that variable's mean. The sign of the deviation reports the direction of that difference (the deviation is positive when the observed value exceeds the reference value). The magnitude of the value indicates the size of the difference.
Interquartile range	In statistics, the interdecile range is the difference between the first and the ninth deciles . The interdecile range is a measure of statistical dispersion of the values in a set of data, similar to the range and the interquartile range, and can be computed from the (non-parametric) seven-number summary. Despite its simplicity, for estimating the standard deviation of a normal distribution, the scaled interdecile range gives a reasonably efficient estimator.
Random variable	In probability and statistics, a random variable, aleatory variable or stochastic variable is a variable whose value is subject to variations due to chance . A random variable can take on a set of possible different values (similarly to other mathematical variables), each with an associated probability (if discrete) or a probability density function (if continuous), in contrast to other mathematical variables. A random variable's possible values might represent the possible outcomes of a yet-to-be-performed experiment, or the possible outcomes of a past experiment whose already-existing value is uncertain (for example, as a result of incomplete information or imprecise measurements).
Range	In arithmetic, the range of a set of data is the difference between the largest and smallest values. However, in descriptive statistics, this concept of range has a more complex meaning. The range is the size of the smallest interval which contains all the data and provides an indication of statistical dispersion.
Degrees of freedom	In many scientific fields, the degrees of freedom of a system is the number of parameters of the system that may vary independently. For example, the position of a figure in the plane has three degrees of freedom: its orientation and the two coordinates of any fixed point of the figure. In mathematics, this notion is formalized as the dimension of a manifold or an algebraic variety.
Error	The word error entails different meanings and usages relative to how it is conceptually applied. The concrete meaning of the Latin word 'error' is 'wandering' or 'straying'. Unlike an illusion, an error or a mistake can sometimes be dispelled through knowledge (knowing that one is looking at a mirage and not at real water does not make the mirage disappear).
Sampling distribution	In statistics, a sampling distribution or finite-sample distribution is the probability distribution of a given statistic based on a random sample.

22. Inferences for Regression

Sampling distributions are important in statistics because they provide a major simplification on the route to statistical inference. More specifically, they allow analytical considerations to be based on the sampling distribution of a statistic, rather than on the joint probability distribution of all the individual sample values.

Standard error

The standard error is the standard deviation of the sampling distribution of a statistic. The term may also be used to refer to an estimate of that standard deviation, derived from a particular sample used to compute the estimate.

For example, the sample mean is the usual estimator of a population mean.

T-statistic

In statistics, the t-statistic is a ratio of the departure of an estimated parameter from its notional value and its standard error. It is used in hypothesis testing, for example in the Student's t-test, in the augmented Dickey-Fuller test, and in bootstrapping.

Power

In physics, power is the rate of doing work. It is equivalent to an amount of energy consumed per unit time. In the MKS system, the unit of power is the joule per second (J/s), known as the watt in honor of James Watt, the eighteenth-century developer of the steam engine.

Hypothesis

A hypothesis is a proposed explanation for a phenomenon. For a hypothesis to be a scientific hypothesis, the scientific method requires that one can test it. Scientists generally base scientific hypotheses on previous observations that cannot satisfactorily be explained with the available scientific theories.

Hypothesis test

A statistical hypothesis test is a method of statistical inference using data from a scientific study. In statistics, a result is called statistically significant if it has been predicted as unlikely to have occurred by chance alone, according to a pre-determined threshold probability, the significance level. The phrase 'test of significance' was coined by statistician Ronald Fisher.

Mean

In probability and statistics, mean and expected value are used synonymously to refer to one measure of the central tendency either of a probability distribution or of the random variable characterized by that distribution. In the case of a discrete probability distribution of a random variable X, the mean is equal to the sum over every possible value weighted by the probability of that value; that is, it is computed by taking the product of each possible value x of X and its probability P(x), and then adding all these products together, giving

$$\mu = \sum x P(x).$$

T-test

A t-test is any statistical hypothesis test in which the test statistic follows a Student's t distribution if the null hypothesis is supported. It can be used to determine if two sets of data are significantly different from each other, and is most commonly applied when the test statistic would follow a normal distribution if the value of a scaling term in the test statistic were known.

22. Inferences for Regression

Logistic regression	In statistics, generalized iterative scaling and improved iterative scaling (IIS) are two early algorithms used to fit log-linear models, notably multinomial logistic regression classifiers and extensions of it such as MaxEnt Markov models and conditional random fields. These algorithms have been largely surpassed by gradient-based methods such as L-BFGS and coordinate descent algorithms.
Extrapolation	In mathematics, extrapolation is the process of estimating, beyond the original observation range, the value of a variable on the basis of its relationship with another variable. It is similar to interpolation, which produces estimates between known observations, but extrapolation is subject to greater uncertainty and a higher risk of producing meaningless results. Extrapolation may also mean extension of a method, assuming similar methods will be applicable.
Regression analysis	The following outline is provided as an overview of and topical guide to regression analysis:
	Regression analysis - in statistics, this includes any technique for learning about the relationship between one or more dependent variables Y and one or more independent variables X.
F-distribution	In probability theory and statistics, the F-distribution is a continuous probability distribution. It is also known as Snedecor's F distribution or the Fisher-Snedecor distribution (after R. A. Fisher and George W. Snedecor). The F-distribution arises frequently as the null distribution of a test statistic, most notably in the analysis of variance; see F-test.
F-test	An F-test is any statistical test in which the test statistic has an F-distribution under the null hypothesis. It is most often used when comparing statistical models that have been fitted to a data set, in order to identify the model that best fits the population from which the data were sampled. Exact 'F-tests' mainly arise when the models have been fitted to the data using least squares.
Statistical significance	Statistical significance is the probability that an effect is not due to just chance alone. It is an integral part of statistical hypothesis testing where it is used as an important value judgment. In statistics, a result is considered significant not because it is important or meaningful, but because it has been predicted as unlikely to have occurred by chance alone.
Confidence interval	In statistical inference, the concept of a confidence distribution has often been loosely referred to as a distribution function on the parameter space that can represent confidence intervals of all levels for a parameter of interest. Historically, it has typically been constructed by inverting the upper limits of lower sided confidence intervals of all levels, and it was also commonly associated with a fiducial interpretation (fiducial distribution), although it is a purely frequentist concept. A confidence distribution is not a valid probability distribution, but may still be a function useful for making inferences.
Contrast	In statistics, particularly analysis of variance and linear regression, an orthogonal contrast is a linear combination of two or more factor level means whose coefficients add up to zero.

22. Inferences for Regression

Non-orthogonal contrasts do not necessarily sum to 0. Contrasts should be constructed 'to answer specific research questions', and do not necessarily have to be orthogonal.

A contrast is defined as the sum of each group mean multiplied by a coefficient for each group (i.e., a signed number, c_j).

Experiment	An experiment is an orderly procedure carried out with the goal of verifying, refuting, or establishing the validity of a hypothesis. Controlled experiments provide insight into cause-and-effect by demonstrating what outcome occurs when a particular factor is manipulated. Controlled experiments vary greatly in their goal and scale, but always rely on repeatable procedure and logical analysis of the results.
Complement	In set theory, a complement of a set A refers to things not in A. The relative complement of A with respect to a set B is the set of elements in B but not in A. When all sets under consideration are considered to be subsets of a given set U, the absolute complement of A is the set of all elements in U but not in A.
One-way ANOVA	In statistics, one-way analysis of variance (abbreviated one-way ANOVA) is a technique used to compare means of two or more samples . This technique can be used only for numerical data.
	The ANOVA tests the null hypothesis that samples in two or more groups are drawn from populations with the same mean values.
Bonferroni method	In statistics, the Holm-Bonferroni method is a method used to counteract the problem of multiple comparisons. It is intended to control the Familywise error rate and offers a simple test uniformly more powerful than the Bonferroni correction. It is one of the earliest usage of stepwise algorithms in simultaneous inference.
Multiple comparisons	In statistics, the multiple comparisons, multiplicity or multiple testing problem occurs when one considers a set of statistical inferences simultaneously or infers a subset of parameters selected based on the observed values. Errors in inference, including confidence intervals that fail to include their corresponding population parameters or hypothesis tests that incorrectly reject the null hypothesis are more likely to occur when one considers the set as a whole. Several statistical techniques have been developed to prevent this from happening, allowing significance levels for single and multiple comparisons to be directly compared.
Theorem	In mathematics, a theorem is a statement that has been proven on the basis of previously established statements, such as other theorems--and generally accepted statements, such as axioms. The proof of a mathematical theorem is a logical argument for the theorem statement given in accord with the rules of a deductive system. The proof of a theorem is often interpreted as justification of the truth of the theorem statement.

22. Inferences for Regression

CHAPTER HIGHLIGHTS & NOTES: KEY TERMS, PEOPLE, PLACES, CONCEPTS

Ordinary least squares	In statistics, ordinary least squares or linear least squares is a method for estimating the unknown parameters in a linear regression model. This method minimizes the sum of squared vertical distances between the observed responses in the dataset and the responses predicted by the linear approximation. The resulting estimator can be expressed by a simple formula, especially in the case of a single regressor on the right-hand side.
Partial regression plot	In applied statistics, a partial regression plot attempts to show the effect of adding an additional variable to the model . Partial regression plots are also referred to as added variable plots, adjusted variable plots, and individual coefficient plots. When performing a linear regression with a single independent variable, a scatter plot of the response variable against the independent variable provides a good indication of the nature of the relationship.
Coefficient	In mathematics, a coefficient is a multiplicative factor in some term of a polynomial, a series or any expression; it is usually a number, but in any case does not involve any variables of the expression. For instance in $7x^2 - 3xy + 1.5 + y$ the first two terms respectively have the coefficients 7 and -3. The third term 1.5 is a constant. The final term does not have any explicitly written coefficient, but is considered to have coefficient 1, since multiplying by that factor would not change the term.
Conditional probability	In probability theory, a conditional probability measures the probability of an event given that another event has occurred. If the events are A and B respectively, this is said to be 'the probability of A given B'. It is commonly denoted by $P(A \backslash B)$, or sometimes $P_B(A)$.
Probability	Probability is a measure of the likeliness that an event will occur. Probability is used to quantify an attitude of mind towards some proposition of whose truth we are not certain. The proposition of interest is usually of the form 'Will a specific event occur?' The attitude of mind is of the form 'How certain are we that the event will occur?' The certainty we adopt can be described in terms of a numerical measure and this number, between 0 and 1 (where 0 indicates impossibility and 1 indicates certainty), we call probability.
Infant mortality	Infant mortality is the death of a child less than one year of age. Childhood mortality is the death of a child before the child's fifth birthday. National statistics tend to group these two mortality rates together.
Independence	In probability theory, to say that two events are independent means that the occurrence of one does not affect the probability of the other. Similarly, two random variables are independent if the realization of one does not affect the probability distribution of the other.

22. Inferences for Regression

1. In mathematics and statistics, _____ is a measure of difference between the observed value of a variable and some other value, often that variable's mean. The sign of the _____ reports the direction of that difference (the _____ is positive when the observed value exceeds the reference value). The magnitude of the value indicates the size of the difference.

   a. Ceiling effect
   b. Cohort
   c. Consistency
   d. Deviation

2. In applied statistics, a _____ attempts to show the effect of adding an additional variable to the model . _____s are also referred to as added variable plots, adjusted variable plots, and individual coefficient plots.

   When performing a linear regression with a single independent variable, a scatter plot of the response variable against the independent variable provides a good indication of the nature of the relationship.

   a. Partial regression plot
   b. Park test
   c. Covariance
   d. Law of total covariance

3. _____ in medicine is a characteristic of diseases to show lighter symptoms without completely disappearing. At a later point, symptoms may return. These symptoms are then called recidive.

   a. 1947 New York City smallpox outbreak
   b. Regression
   c. 2003 Midwest monkeypox outbreak
   d. 2012 Middle East respiratory syndrome coronavirus outbreak

4. A statistical _____ is a method of statistical inference using data from a scientific study. In statistics, a result is called statistically significant if it has been predicted as unlikely to have occurred by chance alone, according to a pre-determined threshold probability, the significance level. The phrase 'test of significance' was coined by statistician Ronald Fisher.

   a. Manhattan Project
   b. Bohr magneton
   c. Bohr model
   d. Hypothesis test

5. . In mathematics, _____ is the process of estimating, beyond the original observation range, the value of a variable on the basis of its relationship with another variable. It is similar to interpolation, which produces estimates between known observations, but _____ is subject to greater uncertainty and a higher risk of producing meaningless results. _____ may also mean extension of a method, assuming similar methods will be applicable.

   a. Extrapolation

b. Rand Corporation

c. Black genocide

d. Definitions of abortion

1. d

2. a

3. b

4. d

5. a

You can take the complete Chapter Practice Test

for 22. Inferences for Regression
on all key terms, persons, places, and concepts.

Online 99 Cents

http://www.JustTheFacts101.com

Use www.JustTheFacts101.com for all your study needs

including Facts101's online interactive problem solving labs in

chemistry, statistics, mathematics, and more.

Other Facts101 e-Books and Tests

Want More?
JustTheFacts101.com...

Jtf101.com provides the outlines and highlights of your textbooks, just like this e-StudyGuide, but also gives you the PRACTICE TESTS, and other exclusive study tools for all of your textbooks.

Learn More. *Just click*
http://www.JustTheFacts101.com/

CPSIA information can be obtained at www.ICGtesting.com
Printed in the USA
BVOW04s1153200814

363453BV00004B/268/P

9 781497 014428